DK EYEWITNESS TOP 10 TRAVEL GUIDES

SICILY

ELAINE TRIGIANI

D0249746

DK PUBLISHING

Left **Greek Theatre, Taormina** Right **Children on the beach**

LONDON, NEW YORK, MUNICH,
MELBOURNE, AND DELHI

Produced by Sargasso Media Ltd, London

Reproduced by Colourscan, Singapore
Printed and bound in Italy by Graphicom

First American Edition, 2003
03 04 05 06 10 9 8 7 6 5 2 3 1

Published in the United States by
DK Publishing, Inc.
375 Hudson Street
New York, New York 10014

ISSN 1479-344X
ISBN 0-7894-9192-3

Within each Top 10 list in this book, no hierarchy
of quality or popularity is implied. All 10 are, in the
editor's opinion, of roughly equal merit.

Floors are referred to throughout in
accordance with European usage; ie the "first
floor" is the floor above ground level.

See our complete product line at
www.dk.com

Contents

Sicily's Top 10

**The information in this
DK Eyewitness Top 10 Travel Guide is checked regularly.**
Every effort has been made to ensure that this book is as up-to-date as possible at the
time of going to press. Some details, however, such as telephone numbers, opening hours,
prices, gallery hanging arrangements and travel information are liable to change.
The publishers cannot accept responsibility for any consequences arising from the use
of this book, nor for any material on third party websites, and cannot guarantee that any
website address in this book will be a suitable source of travel information. We value
the views and suggestions of our readers very highly. Please write to:
Publisher, DK Eyewitness Travel Guides,
Dorling Kindersley, 80 Strand, London WC2R 0RL, Great Britain.

Left **Stromboli, Aeolian Islands** Right **Salt fields, Motya**

Contents

Left **Ragusa** Right **Orecchio di Dioniso, Syracuse**

Key to abbreviations
Adm *admission charge* **Free** *no admission charge* **Dis. access** *disabled access*

SICILY'S
TOP 10

SICILY'S TOP 10

🔟 Sicily's Highlights

The island of Sicily is Italy's largest region and is also its most varied. In terms of geography, there are offshore islands, endless coastline, rugged mountains, rolling wheatfields and volcanos, but its history and architecture are also of note. Sicily formed a significant portion of the Greek empire, was strategically vital to Rome, and was invaded in succession by the Byzantines, Arabs, Normans, French, Spanish and Bourbons, before unifying with Italy. Each conquest left its mark, to create a palimpsest of cultures on the island.

Norman Palermo 1

Norman rule of Sicily only lasted a century, but it left a rich legacy of law, culture and architecture. Their early monuments are grouped around a fortified site in the heart of Palermo *(see pp8–9)*.

Monreale 2

The last and most spectacular of the Norman monuments, the mosaic cycle at Monreale Cathedral is one of the wonders of the medieval world *(see pp10–11)*.

Aeolian Islands 3

Volcanic activity lent to each of these seven islands its own land and seascape. Evidence of 6,000 years of history, a live volcano, black lava beaches, the magnificently limpid sea, and food and wines intensely flavoured by the sun are well worth the trip out *(see pp12–13)*.

Taormina 4

As Sicily's first resort and an obligatory stop on the Grand Tour, Taormina has welcomed visitors for centuries. The town, draped with bougainvillea, offers breathtaking views, an ancient theatre, and cafés and terraces overlooking the sea *(see pp14–15)*.

Mount Etna 5

This, the largest and most active volcano in Europe, has been threatening the island since before records began. Its awesome presence dominates eastern Sicily *(see pp16–17)*.

Syracuse
6 The once mighty Greek colony and rival to Athens quietly exists today as a thriving modern city endowed with vestiges of its former glory *(see pp18–21)*.

Noto
7 Destroyed by an earthquake in 1693, Noto was rebuilt during the 1700s when the Baroque style was at its height. A unified building programme creates harmony between landscape and village *(see pp22–3)*.

3 Aeolian Islands

Milazzo

Capo d'Orlando
Patti
ermini nerese Cefalù San Fratello
Castelbuono Monti Nebrodi Randazzo Taormina **4**
Monti Madonie Caltavuturo
ia Vallelunga Pratameno Nicosia Adrano Mount Etna **5**
Enna Paternò Acireale
ampofranco Caltanissetta Catania
Canicatti **8** Villa Romana del Casale Palagonia
Campobello di Licata Caltagirone Lentini Augusta
Licata Gela Vizzini
Giarratana **6** Syracuse
Vittoria Ragusa
Modica **7** Noto
Scicli Ispica

20 |——— miles ¬0 ┌ km —— ¡20

Villa Romana del Casale
8 The extensive mosaic decorations of this luxurious Roman hunting villa are the best preserved of their kind in the world *(see pp24–5)*.

Agrigento
9 The famed Valle dei Templi is home to ruined Greek temples that stand, or partially stand, against a backdrop of the distant sea. They are as awe-inspiring today as they must have been to the peoples who constructed them 2,500 years ago *(see pp26–9)*.

Selinunte **10**
Another of Sicily's remarkable ancient sites, the romantic remains of Greek Selinus reign spectacularly from a promontory high above the sea. Comprising the largest archaeological park in Europe, Selinunte offers the chance for a solitary ramble among the ruins, walking in the footsteps of history *(see pp30–33)*.

🔟 Norman Palermo

When the Normans entered Palermo in 1071, Count Roger (see p36) favoured living in the Arab fortified palace on the highest point of the city, rather than the former seat of government in La Kalsa (see p82). The building was re-fortified and renamed the Palazzo dei Normanni (Norman Palace). Along with the construction of the church of San Giovanni degli Eremiti and the cathedral, Palermo soon came to represent the Norman architectural and decorative ideal. After centuries of renovations, the cathedral has become uniquely Sicilian in its mix of styles. The Palazzo dei Normanni has also been renovated by successive invaders, but the well-preserved private chapel, where western and Islamic elements are combined, is a jewel.

South porch, Cathedral

⭐ A two-day cumulative ticket (€4.50, reduced to €2.00 for students) gains you entrance to the Church of San Giovanni degli Eremiti, La Zisa and La Cuba *(see p86)*, and Monreale Cathedral *(see pp10–11)*.

• Cathedral: Corso Vittorio Emanuele, Map K5; Open 7am–7pm; interior: Free; Crypt and Treasury: €2.00
• Palazzo dei Normanni: Corso Calatafimi; Map J6; Sala di Re Ruggero: Open 9am–12:30pm Mon, Fri–Sat
• Cappella Palatina: Map J6; Open 9–11:45am, 3–5:45pm Thu–Tue; Free
• San Giovanni degli Eremiti: Map J6; Open 9am–7pm Mon–Sat, 9am–1pm Sun; Adm €4.50

Top 10 Sights

1. Cappella Palatina Interior
2. Cappella Palatina Cupola and Apse Mosaics
3. Cappella Palatina Nave Mosaics
4. Sala di Re Ruggero
5. Cathedral Exterior
6. Cathedral Interior, Norman Tombs
7. Cathedral Treasury and Crypt
8. San Giovanni degli Eremiti Exterior
9. San Giovanni degli Eremiti Cloister
10. San Giovanni degli Eremiti Interior

1 Cappella Palatina Interior

Roger II ordered construction of the Palatine Chapel in 1129, and in 1140 it was dedicated to St Peter. The chapel harmoniously combines western and Arab styles. The Arab ceiling is painted with animals and greenery *(below)* and, surprisingly for Islamic craftsmen, figures.

2 Cappella Palatina Cupola and Apse Mosaics

A Christ Pantocrator, crafted by Greek masters using gold and silver *tesserae*, offers his blessing from the cupola and the apse *(above)*.

3 Cappella Palatina Nave Mosaics

The nave mosaics of Old Testament scenes include Latin inscriptions, indicating that they are the work of Italian artists.

4 Sala di Re Ruggero

Decorated in 1140, this room in the Palazzo dei Normanni is a fine example of secular mosaic decoration *(above)*.

5 Cathedral Exterior

The cathedral was founded by the Archbishop of Palermo in 1185, on the site of a former mosque. Remains of the Norman structure include the exterior of the triple apse and the clock tower.

6 Cathedral Interior, Norman Tombs

Drastically altered in the 1700s, all that remains of the Norman interior are its tombs.

7 Cathedral Treasury and Crypt

The treasury highlight is the crown of Constance of Aragón, encrusted with gemstones and pearls *(above)* crafted in the 12th century. The crypt houses Greek and Roman sarcophagi.

8 San Giovanni degli Eremiti Exterior

Amid its lush gardens *(right)*, the five red domes, characteristic of Arab craftsmen, define the church's exterior.

9 San Giovanni degli Eremiti Cloister

Behind the church is a small cloister *(below)*, built 50 years later and more western in concept. Crumbling pointed arches are supported by a row of twin columns. The quiet space, with a lovely garden setting, provides views to the Palazzo dei Normanni.

Map of Norman Palermo

10 San Giovanni degli Eremiti Interior

Founded in 1132, San Giovanni was the wealthiest monastery in Sicily, but today the interior of the church *(left)* has only a few remains of its original decoration.

The Normans in Sicily

In 1061 the Norman soldier Roger de Hautville took advantage of internal Arab conflict and invaded Sicily with a small number of crusaders. Roger was the first of five Norman kings who, over the following century, succeeded in turning Sicily into a well-run and wealthy monarchy. At the end of their reign, in 1266, they left an island endowed with splendid buildings and an exotic culture that harmoniously blended Arab and western influences.

Monreale

The cathedral at Monreale reigns high above Palermo, on the edge of the fertile Conca d'Oro (Golden Valley). King William II founded the majestic cathedral and Benedictine monastery in 1174, and a medieval village soon grew up around them. Don't be fooled by the rather austere exterior – inside the cathedral is one of the wonders of the medieval world. Its spectacular decoration constitutes the most extensive and important mosaic cycle of its kind. The cathedral faces the lively Piazza Gugliemo, with palm trees and cafés, but the entrance is around to the left in Piazza Vittorio Emanuele, with a fountain in the centre.

Monreale Cathedral from Piazza Gugliemo

🍴 Have a coffee or *gelato* at the Bar Baby O' in Piazza Gugliemo.

✿ The church is popular for weddings – if one is in progress when you visit, go to the cloisters and gardens first and return to the church after the service.

• Piazza Vittorio Emanuele
• Map C2
• 091 640 44 13
• Open 8am–6pm daily, Mass 8am & 5:30pm Mon–Sat, 8:30am, 10:30am, noon & 6pm Sun
• Free
• Cloister: Piazza Gugliemo; 091 640 44 03; Open 9am– 7pm Mon–Sat, 9am–1pm Sun; Adm €4.50.

Top 10 Sights

1. Façade
2. Apse Exterior
3. Interior
4. Ceilings
5. Apse Mosaic of Christ
6. Apse Mosaics of Martyr Saints
7. Side Apse Mosaics
8. Cloister
9. Nave Mosaics
10. Castellaccio

1 Façade
The façade *(above)*, with a bronze door, is bracketed by two asymmetrical square towers and bears decorative stonework. The porch is an 18th-century addition.

2 Apse Exterior
In contrast to the rest of the exterior, which is relatively plain, the triple apse *(right)* is decorated with intricate stonework that forms interlacing arches of limestone and lava. See it from via del Arcivescovado, a short walk around the back of the building.

3 Interior
The interior is not greatly articulated but works as a support for around 6,500 sq m (70,000 sq ft) of brilliant mosaic. The granite columns bear Roman Corinthian capitals.

An added bonus of a visit to Monreale are the stunning views of the valley, extending out to Palermo and the sea in the distance.

4 Ceilings
The choir ceiling shows traces of Arab influences. The nave ceiling was restored after a fire in 1811.

5 Apse Mosaic of Christ
The enormous image of the Christ Pantocrator *(below)* embraces his followers with curved arms and outstretched hands.

8 Cloister
The cloister *(above)* combines Arab-styled arches, intricately carved capitals, and a lovely 12th-century fountain.

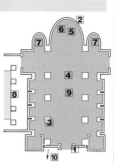

Floorplan of Monreale

10 Castellaccio
The 12th-century Norman castle was once a fortified monastery, but it is now used by the Sicilian Alpine Club. From its hilltop location, the castle commands a view over the valley. It is a pleasant 20-minute walk from town.

6 Apse Mosaics of Martyr Saints
One of the martyr saints represented is St Thomas à Becket, canonized the year before the church was founded. It is his earliest known portrait.

9 Nave Mosaics
These New and Old Testament scenes were educational panels for the illiterate parishioners. They include the Creation, Noah's Ark and the Sacrifice of Isaac.

7 Side Apse Mosaics
Above the thrones to either side of the main apse are portraits of William II being crowned by Christ himself, and presenting the cathedral to the Madonna, a scene blessed by the hand of God. The side apses *(right)* are dedicated to saints Peter and Paul.

King William II
According to legend, in 1174 the Madonna appeared before King William II and led him to the spot where his father had buried a considerable treasure. She instructed him to put it to good use, so William took the opportunity to create a sparkling religious monument to Sicily. Legend aside, William's political rival Walter of the Mill, Archbishop of Palermo, and his faction of landowners and clerics, had become too powerful. In building a cathedral at Monreale (specifically a Benedictine abbey and thus independent of the archbishop), William was able to redistribute the balance of power. The cathedral was finished in just under 10 years. The elaborate mosaic cycle gained fame in its own day.

For more places of worship in Sicily **See pp44–5**

📖 Aeolian Islands

With a mix of history, small town atmosphere, intensely flavoured cuisine, and natural beauty, each of these islands has its own character. Rich in pumice, Lipari is bright white; the fertile volcanic soil of Salina grows verdant grape vines and forest; on Vulcano cooled molten lava has left entire cliffs looking like a row of elephants' legs; while on Salina rock formations rise like mounds of whipped cream. Beaches are white with pumice or black with powdered lava and the sea is clean, clear and full of marine life. The islands' culture extends back 6,000 years, and there is evidence of trade with virtually every important Mediterranean culture, from the Etruscans to the Greeks.

Lipari beach

🍽 Stick to small, unassuming *trattorie* for good food at better prices.

⚠ The islands are made up of fragile volcanic stone so watch out for falling rocks *(cadute masse).*

• Map F1
• Aeolian Archaeological Museum: Lipari Castle; 090 988 01 74; Open 9am–1pm Mon–Sat, Classical Section: 9am–1pm & 3–7pm Mon–Sat; Adm €4.50

Top 10 Sights

1. Aeolian Archaeological Museum, Lipari
2. Marina Corta, Lipari
3. Pumice Quarries, Lipari
4. Pollara Beach, Salina
5. Perciato di Pollara
6. Sulphur Emissions, Vulcano
7. Malvasia delle Lipari
8. Stromboli
9. Panarea
10. Alicudi and Filicudi

1 Aeolian Archaeological Museum, Lipari

The museum's collection reveals the original Neolithic settlement and includes obsidian knives and fabulous Greek vases.

2 Marina Corta, Lipari

Under the castle rock, this is where the hydrofoils and smaller craft dock *(below)*. It's always bustling with visitors and locals hawking rooms for rent and boat excursions.

3 Pumice Quarries, Lipari

The biggest industry on Lipari, alongside tourism, is the thriving pumice industry. Pumice is so plentiful you'll find little bits of it washing up onto the beaches, bobbing in the water and on sale in shops. Thanks to pumice dust on the seabed, the water refracts gorgeous colours, from turquoise to bright emerald.

There are ferries to the islands from Naples, Palermo, Messina, Reggio Calabria and Cefalù.

4 Pollara Beach, Salina

The beach at Pollara *(above)* has black volcanic sand and a dark blue sea. The water is great for snorkelling, with sea urchins and octopuses.

6 Sulphur Emissions, Vulcano

Although it's a spent volcano, Vulcano still has constant sulphur emissions seeping out of the main crater, and all over the island the vapour rises out of the craggy ground. It turns the earth lurid yellows and reds and forms the *fanghi* (mudbaths) and hot bubbles in the sea.

9 Panarea

This is the smallest island of the archipelago and the most exclusive. Chic Panarea *(below)* is known for its coves, clear water, rocky islets and nightlife. It also has an archaeological site: a Bronze Age settlement on the Punta Milazzese.

10 Alicudi and Filicudi

Tiny Alicudi and Filicudi are the westernmost and least developed islands of the archipelago. Many visitors and locals call these the prettiest of the Aeolian Islands, with their natural beauty, sparse population, lack of cars and whitewashed houses with breezy terraces.

5 Perciato di Pollara, Salina

This stone bridge swoops down from the cliff and rests in the water, creating a natural rock bridge *(above)*. You can get to the breathtaking Perciato via land or sea and then swim around the rocks.

7 Malvasia delle Lipari

This is the famed product of the islands. White grapes are cultivated, harvested late and left to shrivel on cane mats before fermentation.

8 Stromboli

Stromboli volcano *(below)* has been active for more than two millennia, spewing sparks and red-hot rocks into the air, although you can only see them at night. Excursions are popular and available from the other islands.

Obsidian and Pumice

The two volcanic by-products obsidian and pumice have played vital roles in Lipari's commerce. The heavy, dense, glass-like black obsidian was crafted into knives and arrowheads in the Neolithic period and was highly valued and widely traded. The quarrying of white, porous pumice is the major industry at Lipari, where the enormous quarries grind the rock for use in a variety of industries worldwide.

Taormina

On a spectacular site on Monte Tauro, with views of the rocky coastline, the blue-green sea and the breathtaking Mount Etna, Tauromenium was founded in 304 BC as a colony of powerful Syracuse. The town endured a typical Sicilian history, falling first to the Romans, then to the Arabs, Normans and Spanish. However, during the 1800s it became an obligatory stop on The Grand Tour and life changed forever – Taormina has been host to foreign visitors ever since and, unlike much of the island, is well equipped to cater to them. The plethora of hotels, restaurants and shops, as well as beaches and manicured gardens, makes it Sicily's most popular holiday destination.

View of Taormina

🍴 Stop at the Grand Hotel Timeo (via Teatro Greco) on the way to the theatre for a drink or dinner on their splendid terrace.

• Map H3
• Greek Theatre: Via Teatro Greco, 0942 23220, Open 9am–7pm daily, Adm €4.50

Top 10 Sights

1 Greek Theatre
2 View and Acoustics
3 Corso Umberto I
4 Piazza Vittorio Emanuele
5 Piazza IX Aprile
6 Borgo Medievale
7 Piazza del Duomo
8 Giardino Pubblico
9 Castelmola Walk
10 Mazzarò Walk

Greek Theatre 1
Carved out of the hillside, the theatre seen today *(right)* was refurbished by the Romans in the 1st century AD. They sacrificed some of the seats and part of the stage to make a circular arena to accommodate gladiator games.

View and Acoustics 2
The Greeks designed the theatre in the 3rd century BC, with the spectacular view *(above)* forming a backdrop to their plays. Praised for its acoustics, from the top you can eavesdrop on fellow visitors at stage level.

Corso Umberto I 3
The people of Taormina make their *passeggiata* (nightly stroll) here on the Corso, beginning at Porta Messina and crossing several lively piazzas towards the end at Porta Catania. Enjoy the plentiful bars, *gelaterie*, shops and crowds.

Piazza Vittorio Emanuele 4
This piazza boasts the Palazzo Corvaja, an architectural hybrid of Arab, Norman and Catalan Gothic elements (now a tourist office), and the Santa Caterina church backed by Roman ruins.

5 Piazza IX Aprile
On this lovely square *(above)* you are spoilt for choice between the sea views and people-watching at the many outdoor cafés. The Wunderbar plays live music in the evenings.

7 Piazza del Duomo
The Baroque fountain in the piazza bears a centaur, the symbol of Taormina, here atypically female. The 13th-century Chiesa Madre, dedicated to San Nicolò, has six ancient marble columns and a tree of life relief carving.

Map of Taormina

9 Castelmola Walk
From via Circonvallazione take the "Salita Castello" path to the summit of Monte Tauro to enjoy the views and the medieval castle ruins.

10 Mazzarò Walk
Below Taormina are beaches, grottoes, coves and the tiny Isola Bella *(above)*, attached to the coast by a strip of sand.

6 Borgo Medievale
The clocktower *(above)* is the gateway to the medieval part of town. The Corso is narrower here, and while the shops are the same mix of clothing and souvenirs, the shopfronts have kept their medieval character.

8 Giardino Pubblico
With views down to Giardini Naxos *(see p100)*, the well-tended public gardens *(below)* have palm and banana trees, birds of paradise, exotic plants, a monument to Taormina's sailors and many whimsical buildings.

Famous Visitors

Of the innumerable well known names that have revelled in Taormina's beauty throughout its history are: Greek king, Pyrrhus (318–272 BC); Norman conqueror Count Roger *(see p36)*; German poet Johann Wolfgang Goethe (1749–1832); English novelist D.H. Lawrence (1885–1930); Kaiser Wilhelm of Germany (1859–1941); American playwright Tennessee Williams (1911–83); English author Roald Dahl (1916–90); and Hollywood movie stars Elizabeth Taylor and Richard Burton.

Reach Mazzarò via a steep path with steps or take the funivia (cable car) from the station in via L. Pirandello.

🔟 Mount Etna

Dominating the eastern side of the island, Mount Etna is Europe's largest volcano, with several vast craters and a height of 3,330 m (10,925 ft), and it remains one of the world's most active. To the Greeks, it was home to Hephaestus, god of fire, who used its flames and lava to forge Zeus's thunderbolts; to the Arabs it was known as Mongibello (Mountain of Mountains). Today, the Parco dell'Etna encompasses much of the volcano, encouraging farmers to produce wine, cheese, honey and fruit in the rich lavic soil. For visitors, it offers breathtaking views, great hiking and, in season, skiing – and you just might see an eruption of bright red sparks and lava.

View of Mount Etna

🍃 Follow hiking and safety guidelines provided by the park service – guided tours are recommended. If you set out without a guide, check in first with the park service to advise them of your route. Bring warm clothing, sturdy shoes and glasses to protect your eyes from blowing grit.

- Map G3
- Parco dell' Etna: 095 914 588
- Circumetnea train: 095 543 232
- Rifugio Sapienza: 095 914 141; minibus and guide; €37.00

Top 10 Sights

1. Circumetnea Train
2. Vegetation
3. Fauna
4. Southern and Western Slopes
5. Eastern and Northern Slopes
6. Summit Craters
7. Visitor Centres
8. Lava Flows
9. Valle del Bove
10. Hikes

1 Circumetnea Train
From Catania, the train *(above)* passes Adrano (site of a Saracen bridge), Bronte (pistachio farms), Randazzo (Lake Gurrida and lava flows) and Linguaglossa (murals). Stop at Nicolosi and Zafferana for walks to the crater or the lava flows.

2 Vegetation
Etna is home to a variety of trees, from oak and chestnut in low areas, to pine and birch on higher slopes. Wildflowers including violets *(right)*, flourish in the lavic soil.

3 Fauna
Development has all but eliminated Etna's wolves, wild boar and deer, but small species still thrive, such as weasels and wildcats.

4 Southern and Western Slopes
Small volcanic cones and cultivated crops, notably pistachio, cover the western slopes. Recent lava flows can be seen on the south slopes.

There are jeep tours from the cable car station to 2,800 m (9,180 ft), 9am–5pm daily. Includes a summit alpine tour (€38.00).

5 Eastern and Northern Slopes

On these slopes can be found the *Betula aetnensis* birch, unique to the woods of Mount Etna, and the *Castagno dei Cento Cavalli* (Chestnut of 100 Horses), one of the oldest and largest trees in the world. Lava flows have formed caves and grottoes, used as shelter and ice stores.

8 Lava Flows

Molten lava *(above)* is more than 500° C (930° F). In places, the constant flow, 2 m (6.5 ft) underfoot, causes the snow to melt.

Map of Mount Etna

10 Hikes

Hikes on lower slopes and towards the crater are possible *(above)*, safety permitting. Tourist offices provide maps and guides.

Recent Eruptions

In 1928, lava wiped out coastal Mascali (the only town destroyed in the 20th century), vast tracts of farm land and 550 buildings. The 1950s, 1960s and 1970s brought danger to Milo, Fornazzo, Zafferana and Sant'Alfio. A massive eruption in 1979 killed nine tourists. Between 1991 and 1993 Italian and American forces dropped huge concrete blocks from helicopters to stop lava near Zafferana. In 1999–2000 ash covered Catania, closing the airport and roads. Lava flows from the October 2002 eruption approached Linguaglossa and destroyed visitors' centres and hotels at Piano Provenzano.

6 Summit Craters

The summit height is constantly in flux due to mounting volcanic debris ejected during explosions and frequent landslides. The Central Crater, the Northeast Crater and the Southeast Crater emit a constant stream of sulphuric gas *(above)*.

9 Valle del Bove

This crater *(below)* was created by partial collapse of the volcano wall. It covers 7 km by 5 km (4.5 miles by 3 miles) and has walls more than 1,000 m (3,000 ft) high. In 1991 a vent opened, releasing lava into the valley for two years.

7 Visitor Centres

Jeep tours start at the Rifugio Sapienza Etna Sud near the Monti Silvestri, and just above the Monte Vetore. They follow the cable car line, destroyed in the 2001 eruption, as far as seismic activity allows. Guides are provided.

For more on Mount Etna's historic eruptions See p104

🔟 Syracuse

Founded in 733 BC by Corinthian settlers, Syracusae became one of the first Greek colonies on the island. It quickly attained wealth and power, commissioned important buildings, works of art, and founded sub-colonies, extending its territory through warfare to become the strongest city in the Mediterranean. The ancient city was up to three times the size of Syracuse today and was divided into five zones: the sparsely populated Epipolae, the necropolis zone of Akradina, residential Tyche, Neapolis (where the theatre is located), and the island of Ortygia, the original settlement.

Grotto, Latomia del Paradiso

🍽 The cafés on Ortygia come alive at sundown. Enjoy the relaxed atmosphere and cool sea breeze.

🎫 Cumulative tickets (€6.00) are available for the archaeological museum and park.

- Map H5
- Parco Archeologico: Viale Augusto; 0931 66 206, Open 9am–6pm daily; Adm €4.50
- Catacombs of San Giovanni: Piazza S Giovanni; 339 10 22 077; Open 9am–1pm, 2:30–5:30pm Tue–Sun; Adm €3.50
- Museo Regionale Archeologico "Paolo Orsi": Viale Teocrito 66; 0931 46 40 22; Open 9am–Sun, 3:30–6:30pm Mon, Wed, Sat; Adm €4.50
- Castle of Euryalus: 8 km (5 miles) from Syracuse; Bus No. 11; 0931 711 773; Open 9am–1 hr before sunset; Free

Top 10 Sights

1. Latomia del Paradiso
2. Greek Theatre
3. Cavea
4. Nymphaeum and Street of Tombs
5. Altar of Hieron II
6. Roman Amphitheatre
7. Catacombs of San Giovanni
8. Necropoli Grotticelli
9. Museo Archeologico Regionale "Paolo Orsi"
10. Castle di Eurialo

1 Latomia del Paradiso

Stone from this *latomia* (quarry) was used entirely for the construction of Syracuse. Within the quarry is the *Orecchio di Dioniso* (Ear of Dionysius) cavern (*above*), which may have got its name from its large opening resembling a human ear.

2 Greek Theatre

Begun in the 6th century BC, the Greek Theatre (*above*) became the largest theatre in Sicily. Many of Aeschylus's tragedies were first staged here, including *Prometheus Bound*.

3 Cavea

The *cavea* (seating area) of the theatre was hewn out of rock and accommodated 15,000 spectators. Its size is still impressive today.

4 Nymphaeum and Street of Tombs

The *Nymphaeum* (grotto) was fed with water from an aqueduct. To the left is the Street of Tombs, an ancient street filled with votive niches and Byzantine graves.

Performances of Prometheus Bound and other classical plays are still staged at the Greek Theatre See p63

Map of Syracuse

5 Altar of Hieron II
Hieron II built this immense altar *(above)*, the largest in Magna Graecia, around 225 BC and dedicated it to Zeus Eleutherios, the god of freedom. Today, only the base remains.

10 Castle di Eurialo
The castle is the most important extant Greek military installation, built by Dionysus the Younger in the 4th century BC and later improved by Hieron II. Defensive trenches *(above)* can be accessed.

6 Roman Amphitheatre
The arena *(below)* was built in the 3rd century AD and is one of the largest of its kind, built by local stonemasons.

7 Catacombs of San Giovanni
Throughout these vast limestone catacombs are burial chambers varying in size to accommodate children, adults or families.

8 Necropoli Grotticelli
At the eastern end of one of the quarries is a large necropolis where many tomb chambers were carved out of the limestone. At the corner of via Teracati is the so-called Tomb of Archimedes, used for holding funerary urns.

9 Museo Archeologico Regionale "Paolo Orsi"
Named after the archaeologist Paolo Orsi, the museum specializes in the Greek artifacts he and other scientists found during digs in Syracuse *(see pp20–21)*.

Archimedes
Archimedes (287–212 BC) the renowned mathematician, engineer and inventor, was born in Syracuse and educated in Alexandria. Among his important discoveries is Archimedes Principle, the study of a body's displacement of its weight in water. He put many of his other inventions, such as the pulley and catapult, to use in war machines and defensive mechanisms when requested to act as military advisor to Hieron II. He was killed during the Second Punic War by a Roman soldier.

Left **Villa Landolina Gardens** Right **Gargoyles from the Temple of Athena**

🔟 Archaeology Museum Highlights

1 Villa Landolina Gardens

Villa Landolina's gardens sit on a site rich in finds from an ancient Greek necropolis, parts of Hellenistic streets and later Christian catacombs.

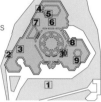

Museum Floorplan

2 Bronze Age Material from Castelluccio

Materials from the Castelluccio site, between Noto and Palazzolo Acreide, show trade links between early Sicilians and eastern Mediterranean cultures.

3 Material from Pantalica

Pantalica, near Palazzolo Acreide, was inhabited by the pre-Greek Sicels, who produced elegant red-glazed pottery.

4 Greek Kouros, Lentini

This 6th-century BC *kouros* (statue of a muscular youth) is one of the best examples of ancient Greek sculpture.

Bronze Age pottery

5 Mother Goddess

Made of terracotta around 500 BC, this object represents the mother goddess nursing twins. She is remarkable for the sense of solidity blended with tenderness.

6 Venus Anadyomene

A Roman copy of a Greek 2nd-century BC original. From her pose, to the high polish of the marble, she is an image of pure sensuality.

7 Temples of Athena and Apollo

Fragments from two Doric temples on Ortygia are on show, such as polychrome parts of a Gorgon.

8 Ephebus from Adrano

This small athletic bronze figure was found near Adrano, and dates from around 460 BC.

9 Gela Vase Collection

A *lekythoi* (tall one-handed vase) painted with *Herakles and the Hydra* is the most impressive.

10 Wooden Statuettes of Demeter and Kore

These rare examples of wooden statuary were found at a sanctuary between Gela and Agrigento. They date from the late 7th century BC and survived because they were covered in the mineral-rich mud of a local spring.

The History of Ancient Syracuse

Under the tyrant Gelon, Syracuse formed a mighty alliance with other Greeks at Akragas (Agrigento) and Gela and defeated the Carthaginians at Himera in 180 BC. Subsequent tyrants such as Hieron I (478–466 BC) and Dionysius (405–367 BC) made Syracuse the most powerful city on the island and in the Mediterranean. In 413 BC Athens sent a well-equipped fleet in what is known as the Great Expedition to put down the threat from what it saw as an upstart colony; with help from Sparta, the Athenians were sorely defeated. Despite their war-lord image, Syracuse's rulers were patrons of the arts – Hieron II (265–215 BC) expanded the great theatre and Aeschylus, Pindar, Plato and Plutarch were present at court. But the end was in sight. After Hieron II's death, Syracuse sided not with Rome but with Carthage in the Second Punic Wars. After a siege lasting two years, Syracuse fell to Rome in 211 BC and began a slow decline, made final in AD 878 when the city was burned by the Arabs. Syracuse never again attained the importance it had held for centuries.

Excavating the Past

Extensive archaeological digs on the site of ancient Syracuse have been successful in uncovering remnants of that great colony such as this 5th-century BC bust *(left)* and numerous pre-Greek vases and urns *(below)*.

TOP 10 Noto

Noto is proud of its ancient origins – it was from Neas, as Noto was then known, that the Sicilian leader Ducetius led rebellions against the Greeks (see p36). After the massive earthquake that destroyed almost all of eastern Sicily in 1693, major reconstruction resulted in cities and villages being designed in the Baroque style, then at the height of popularity, and Noto is one of the best examples. Designed specifically to include vistas of the countryside, the urban plan was sensitive to the needs of the citizens and still works well today. The soft, locally quarried stone adapted well to the carved decorations, but not, unfortunately, to the elements – recent renovation has been necessary.

Balcony, Palazzo Nicolaci

🍴 Drop into the Caffè Sicilia, on the Corso next to San Carlo, to sample wonderful Sicilian pastries and *gelati* made from the best local ingredients.

• Map G5
• Tourist Office: Piazza XXIV Maggio (under San Domenico); 0931 573 779, Open 8:30am–2pm, 3:30–6:30pm daily (closed Sun pm)

Top 10 Sights

1. Porta Reale
2. Chiesa di Santa Chiara & Santissimo Salvatore
3. Piazza Municipio, Palazzo Ducezio
4. Cattedrale di San Nicolò
5. San Carlo al Corso
6. Chiesa di San Domenico
7. Chiesa di Montevergini
8. Palazzi, Via Cavour
9. Old Market, Via Rocco Pirri
10. Chiesa del SS Crocifisso

1 Porta Reale
The Royal Gate was erected in 1838 to greet King Ferdinand II. It offers a grand entrance to Corso Vittorio Emanuele, Noto's main street *(above)*.

2 Chiesa di Santa Chiara & Santissimo Salvatore
On opposite sides of the street are the convent of Santa Chiara and the monastery of Santissimo Salvatore. Santa Chiara's oval interior houses a 16th-century *Madonna and Child* sculpted by Sicilian Antonello Gagini.

3 Piazza Municipio, Palazzo Ducezio
The lovely town square is home to the Palazzo Ducezio, now the town hall *(below)*, designed by Sinatra in 1742. A dramatic, recessed loggia runs the length of the façade.

If you enjoy people-watching, don't miss the Sunday morning, after-church passeggiata along the Corso and Piazza Municipio.

4 Cattedrale di San Nicolò

The cathedral sits on top of Labisi's grand staircase and was built in stages throughout the 18th century with input from both Gagliardi and Sinatra. The façade is flanked by two square towers decorated with Corinthian pilasters. The cupola collapsed in 1996 but is under repair.

6 Chiesa di San Domenico

Gagliardi's masterpiece (1737) has an exuberant, convex façade (*left and above*) which pulsates with niches and columns creating dramatic contrasts of light and shade.

7 Chiesa di Montevergini

Looking up via Nicolaci, this elegantly simple church (*below*), with its concave façade, theatrically marks the end of the street. Nearby is Palazzo Nicolaci, known for its decorated balconies supported by carved horses and grotesques.

9 Old Market, Via Rocco Pirri

Noto's lively market was at one time held in this courtyard, but sadly, butchers and bakers have now been replaced by boutiques. However, there is a market in town every Monday across from San Domenico (*below*).

10 Chiesa del SS Crocifisso

The unfinished church in Noto Alta (Upper Noto), is a sombre Gagliardi design of 1715. It contains many works of art, notably *Madonna della Neve* signed by Francesco Laurana in 1471.

Baroque Architecture

The Baroque style evolved from the Renaissance, which employed Classical forms and primary shapes to create balance and proportion. Baroque architects applied these forms to curved and ovoid shapes to achieve movement and drama. Trademarks are an elliptical floorplan, a façade that projects outward or undulates, use of light and shade, concave forms, and exuberant decoration. Sicilians, in typical fashion, melded Italian Baroque with other cultures and made it their own.

5 San Carlo al Corso

Built in 1730, the church greets visitors with its graceful concave façade. The orders of the wonderfully elegant columns, with their swollen middles, progress up the façade: Doric to Ionic and finally Corinthian. The octagonal dome is silhouetted against the sky; climb up to the top for beautiful views over the town.

8 Palazzi, Via Cavour

Via Cavour is lined with *palazzi* of noble families. The Palazzo Trigona is a stately Baroque design of 1781 with characteristically curved balconies and a frescoed interior. On the corner to the left is Palazzo Battaglia, a late Baroque work by Gagliardi, and further down on the right is the Neo-Classical Palazzo Castelluccio.

🔟 Villa Romana del Casale

As the hunting lodge of an important Roman official (perhaps Maximianus, Diocletian's co-emperor), the villa at Piazza Armerina was decorated with what is now the best preserved and most extensive set of Roman mosaics in the world. The lavish villa was constructed over a period of more than 50 years from the late 3rd century to the early 4th century AD and its public and private rooms, peristyles, luxurious thermal baths and gardens with pools and fountains were laid out on four natural terraces. The villa entrance was an imitation triumphal arch, while inside, the house was endowed with tall ceilings and expansive rooms with open porticoes of delicate marble columns.

Garden, Villa Romana del Casale

🕐 Do your best to arrive as close as possible to opening hours or around lunchtime to avoid the crowds.

The Private Apartments are currently closed for restoration.

- Map F4
- 0935 680 036
- Open 8am–7:30pm daily
- Adm €4.50

Top 10 Features

1. Narthex of the Thermae
2. Private Entrance into Thermae
3. Public Room off the Peristyle
4. Great Hunting Scene
5. Ten Girls in Bikinis
6. Xystus
7. Triclinium
8. Arion and Naiads
9. Private Apartments
10. Aqueduct

1 Narthex of the Thermae

The long narthex in the *thermae* (gym) is decorated with a circus scene *(above)*. Horse-drawn chariots careen around a track, in the centre of which is an image of the obelisk of Constantinus II.

2 Private Entrance into Thermae

Here the emperor's family is shown: mother, son and daughter, accompanied by their slaves, are carrying equipment they will need for the baths and gym *(right)*.

3 Public Room off the Peristyle

The reception room is decorated with a hunting scene – one of the earliest mosaics laid down in the villa. Hunters and their dogs chase beasts, finally spearing a wild boar, carting him away on their shoulders.

4 Great Hunting Scene
These mosaics show two countries (personified at either end) surrounded by sea. The array of animals on land *(above)* and in the sea is astounding – including elephants, lions and tigers, and a leopard attacking a gazelle.

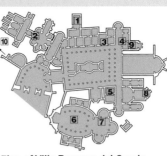

Plan of Villa Romana del Casale

5 Ten Girls in Bikinis
Perhaps the most famous mosaics in the villa *(below)*. The bikini-clad athletes have apparently just finished a competition and the winner has been awarded a flowered crown and a palm sceptre.

6 Xystus
On the north side of the *xystus*, the elliptical garden off the *triclinium (left)*, are three rooms decorated with scenes of the *vendemmia* (grape harvest); the rooms on the south side are decorated with fishing scenes.

7 Triclinium
The triclinium, used for banqueting, opens on one side onto a lovely garden surrounded by an elliptical portico. The mosaics *(above)* are of a grand scale in keeping with their subject, the Ten Labours of Hercules.

8 Arion and Naiads
The floor of this living room, which had marble-faced walls, is decorated with a lively scene of the bejewelled Arion, holding a conch shell as a sceptre. She is surrounded by Niads and sea creatures, all in fine detail.

9 Private Apartments
The floors of the family's private apartments are decorated with scenes of a children's hunt. Lush decorative panels throughout depict foliage and baskets of fruit and vegetables.

10 Aqueduct
Near the entrance to the villa notice remains of the aqueduct, which provided ample water not only for the baths, but also for the extensive gardens, fountains and household use.

Mosaics
The Villa Romana's mosaic floors are almost perfectly preserved because the house was buried under a mudslide in the 12th century. The mosaic artist (possibly North African) was extremely skilled in his craft, assembling millions of tiny polychrome tiles *(tesserae)* to form large-scale images to completely cover more than 3,500 sq m (37,670 sq ft) of floor space. Usually only the most important rooms of the house were decorated, with a flat geometric border and perhaps one small image in the centre of a room.

🔟 Agrigento and the Valle dei Templi

Aligned with Syracuse, Greek Akragas took part in defeating the Carthaginians at Himera in 480 BC. The town boasted a population of around 200,000, constructed temples to its gods, and was known for breeding horses, with which it consistently won the Olympic Games. After being besieged by the Carthaginians in 406 BC, the town was taken by the Romans in 261 BC, renamed Agrigentum, and remained in Roman control until the fall of the Empire. Subsequent versions of Agrigento were built above the acropolis of the ancient city, now known as the Valle dei Templi (Valley of the Temples). Views of the ruins, set on rugged landscape and backed by the sea, are an unmissable sight.

Gigante, Temple of Olympian Zeus

🚫 Avoid the crowded restaurants at the temple site and have a meal in town *(see p115).*

⏱ If you plan to see both the archaeological site and the museum, ask for a combined ticket – it won't be offered automatically.

• Map D4
• Valle dei Templi: 0922 497 341; Open 8:30am–8pm daily; Adm €4.50
• Archaeological Museum: Via dei Templi; 0922 401 565; Open 9am–1pm Sun–Mon, 9am–1:30pm, 2–7pm Tue–Sat; Adm €4.50

Top 10 Sights

1. Centro Storico
2. Abbazia di Santo Spirito
3. Temple of Herakles
4. Temple of Concord
5. Temple of Hera
6. Temple of Olympian Zeus
7. Sanctuary of the Chthonic Deities
8. Greek Roads, Gates & Walls
9. San Nicola
10. Hellenistic/Roman Quarter

1 Centro Storico
Pass through the historic centre to get to the Duomo, walking up from Via Ateneo via alleyways *(above)* and passing artisans' workshops and women pausing from their daily chores to chat.

2 Abbazia di Santo Spirito
The abbey *(right)* dates from around 1290 and the resident Cistercian nuns still practise the centuries-old tradition of pastry-making, which was once the exclusive work of the convents.

3 Temple of Herakles
Amid olive and almond trees lie the ruins of this hexastyle temple dating from around 500 BC. It is the oldest of the temples still standing in Agrigento. Cross over the ancient street and walk over the stones to see the parts of the *cella* wall and Doric columns – particularly beautiful at sunset.

→ At Abbazia di Santo Spirito you can buy a selection of their homemade biscuits with almonds and pistachios for €8.00.

Temple of Concord

The hexastyle Temple of Concord *(above and below)* remains intact because it was usurped for use as a church. It dates from 430 BC.

Sanctuary of the Chthonic Deities

There are various jumbled remains of what was the walled sanctuary of the underground earth goddesses Demeter and her daughter Persephone.

Map of Agrigento and the Valle dei Templi

San Nicola

The front of the church has an interesting 13th-century portal that incorporates materials from a Roman ruin, and a nicely arched interior in plain stone.

10 Hellenistic/ Roman Quarter

Among knee-high ruins make out basins, columns, door jambs in walls, mills, steps, remains of the elaborate drainage system, and mosaic flooring in geometric designs.

Temple of Hera

Patches of red at this temple to the queen of the gods (c.450 BC) indicate fire damage, perhaps from the Carthaginian siege of 406 BC.

Temple of Olympian Zeus

This jumble of massive stones *(below)* is all that remains of what was the largest known Greek temple in the world.

Greek Roads, Gates & Walls

Walking from temple to temple throughout the valley one can see what is left of the infrastructure of the Greek city: roads with ruts, and city walls *(above)* bearing the marks from later ages, when gaps were carved in to them to make room for new Byzantine tombs and gates.

Valle dei Templi Guide

The site is divided into three distinct sections, all of which are near a central car park with ticket booth and tourist information office. The Temple of the Olympian Zeus and the Sanctuary of the Chthonic Deities are in an area just to the west of the car park. The entrance to the temples along the via Sacra (Herakles, Hera and Concord) is just across the street. Just up the via dei Templi towards town are the museum entrance *(see pp28–9)* to the left and and the entrance to the Hellenistic/Roman Quarter on the right.

San Nicola is only open for weddings, but Sicilian weddings are frequent, so feel free to quietly have a look inside.

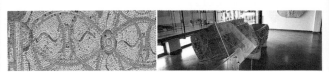

Left **Roman Quarter mosaic** Right **Sarcophagus of a Child**

🔟 Archaeological Museum Exhibits

1 Head of a Bull
Materials excavated from both Agrigento and Gela are found in the first two galleries. They include Bronze Age pots painted with red geometric designs, locally produced pottery, as well as Greek finds. One of the most interesting is the little head of a bull, hand-moulded in pinched terracotta.

2 Vase Collection
The vase collection includes outstanding examples of Attic black-figure and red-figure vases as well as Hellenistic vases. The *krater* (a tall vase with a sturdy base and two handles), with a rare white background, shows the figures of Perseus and Andromeda.

3 Lion-Head Water Spouts
Recovered from various temples at Agrigento, (including the Temples of Herakles and Demeter), these spouts, shaped like lions' heads, were originally placed along the roof of temples, just above the cornice, to funnel rain water to the ground. Note that they were painted in bright colours, as were all of the elements of the temple above the level of the column capitals.

4 Temple of Olympian Zeus Model
This reconstruction of the largest known Greek temple *(see p27)* helps us understand its once enormous size. Note the position of the 8-m (26-ft) tall *gigante* (giant stone figures) in relation to the massive columns. More than twice as tall, the temple's columns measured 16.5 m (54 ft) and had a diameter of 4 m (13 ft) at their base.

5 Gigante and Gigante Heads
Thirty-eight *gigante* once supported the entablature of the Temple of Olympian Zeus. A

Vase Collection

complete figure was reconstructed in the 1800s from various parts found on the site. Each figure was composed of several stones, covered with a smooth stucco overlay, and probably colour as well. Scholars still debate the exact form and position of the *gigante*, but it may be that they stood with feet splayed.

6 Ephebus of Agrigento
Described as an *Ephebus* (a youth taking part in a religious rite), this beautifully carved marble figure illustrates the transition from the static archaic style to the severe style. Note the fine modelling of the boy's musculature and the movement of the figure, which dramatically contrasts to the almost Egyptian-like stilted and stiff figures of the former archaic style.

7 Roman Quarter Mosaics
These particularly fine Roman mosaics from the 2nd century AD are made of tiny *tesserae* (tiles). They served as centrepieces to the decorative mosaic flooring of houses in the residential sector of the city.

8 Sarcophagus of a Child
Dating from the 2nd century BC, this sarcophagus was only discovered in the 1970s. The panels, carved in high relief, illustrate scenes from the child's life and a detailed scene of the sick room, with the father pulling his beard in mourning.

9 Greek and Roman Helmets
Found in Eraclea Minoa, the fascinating Greek battle helmets are designed with ear

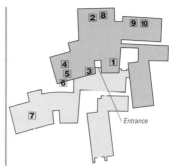

Archaeological Museum Floorplan

holes, while the Roman ones have a top knot and finely chased rims.

10 Red-figure Krater
The "Battle of the Amazons" (c.460 BC) design on this striking *krater* vase has been attributed to the Niobid painter. The artist skilfully created space on the curved surface by illustrating fallen bodies, bows and arrows, and other battlefield paraphernalia in rough perspective. The main scene shows Achilles killing an Amazon queen (and falling in love with her as he does so).

Gigante

Selinunte

The ruins of ancient Selinunte (Selinus), once a large settlement at the westernmost reaches of Magna Graecia, loom high on a promontory above the sparkling Mediterranean. Now one of the most important archaeological sites in Europe, it boasts one of the largest Greek temples in the world. Selinunte was founded in 628 BC and enjoyed centuries of prosperity before being reduced to rubble by the Carthaginians during the First Punic War. The city was later totally abandoned (see p33), but its solid yet graceful Doric temples stand out against the bright blue sky, offering a glimpse of its former grandeur.

Acropolis ruins

🏊 A stunning view of the ruins can be had if you swim out from the beach at Marinella and look to your right.

🎫 The tourist office at Castelvetrano organizes events in the park from mid-July until the end of August. Enjoy a picnic dinner amid the ruins watching ancient myths, classical dance or modern music. Check at the ticket booth for details.

• Marinella di Selinunte, state road 115 south of Castelvetrano
• Map B4
• 0924 46 277
• Open 9am–1 hour before sunset (purchase tickets up to 2 hours before sunset)
• Adm €4.13

Top 10 Sights

1. East Group of Temples
2. Temple G
3. Fortified Acropolis Walls
4. Acropolis
5. Temples A and O
6. Temple C
7. Commercial Area and Stoa
8. North Gate
9. Sanctuary of Malophorus
10. Metopes

1 East Group of Temples
Here lie the ruins of three temples on which decorative fragments are identifiable. Re-erected in modern times, Temple E is an example of balanced Doric order.

2 Temple G
The only octastyle temple at Selinunte (all others are hexastyle), Temple G *(above)* is one of the four largest Greek temples in the world. Its columns alone are more than 16 m (52 ft) high. It was left unfinished in 480 BC – note some unfluted columns.

3 Fortified Acropolis Walls
The original walls, built of large blocks of stone, were reinforced after the city was sacked by Carthage in 409 BC, and a second circle built around 305 BC.

4 Acropolis
The promontory was levelled by the first settlers, allowing them to build sacred buildings; commercial and residential structures followed.

5 Temples A and O
Temple A and its twin, Temple O, of which only the base remains, were built in Doric style around 480 BC, making them the most recent ruins on the site.

6 Temple C
Built on a rise, this was the most important temple *(above)*. It was decorated with polychrome stone and terracotta elements.

Plan of Selinunte

9 Sanctuary of Malophorus
This funerary sanctuary dedicated to Malophorus, the pomegranate-bearing goddess, was in use from the 7th to the 3rd centuries BC.

10 Metopes
Selinunte's *metopes* with scenes from Greek mythology are now found in the Archaeological Museum in Palermo *(see p82)*. The carved *metopes* from Temples E and F are outstanding examples of Classical style.

Selinunte Orientation

Selinunte was built on hilltops around the mouths of the Cotone and Selinon (now Modione) rivers. From the main car park, with ticket booth, a path leads to the East Group of Temples. The Acropolis is located across the valley (location of the old harbour) and is accessible on foot or by car; the second car park is at its base. The sanctuary of Malophorus, reached by walking west from the Acropolis, is not accessible to private vehicles. The large residential section of Selinunte lies to the north of the Acropolis but it is not open to the general public.

8 North Gate
Of great importance for the defence of Selinunte, the 7-m (23-ft) high North Gate *(below)* was protected by a sophisticated fortification composed of three bastions and a double line of walls. After sustaining damage in 409 BC, the earlier ring of walls was reinforced.

7 Commercial Area and Stoa
Behind Temple D you can see remains of shops, each with two rooms, a courtyard and stairs that led to the shopkeepers' apartments on the upper floors. At the east corner are remains of a *stoa*, or colonnaded marketplace *(above)*.

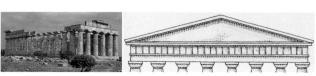

Left **Temple E, Selinunte** Right **Pediment**

Features of a Doric Temple

1 Proportion
Greek architecture followed rules of proportion to ensure the beauty and harmony of the finished structure. Doric temples were built with a length to width ratio of 3:1 or 2:1. Column height was related proportionally to base diameter, with columns gradually becoming more slender over the centuries.

2 Columns
Doric columns are comprised of a simple capital and a fluted shaft without a base. The shaft is larger in diameter at the bottom than at the top, swelling out slightly in the middle *(entasis)*.

3 Colonnade
Columns are arranged around the outer edge of the temple's *crepidoma* (base) forming a colonnade. Peripteral refers to a single colonnade and dipteral to a double colonnade.

4 Entablature
The entablature rests above the capitals and below the pediment.

5 Frieze
This is the decorative feature of the entablature. It is made up of alternating triglyphs – grooved blocks ending in little teeth *(guttae)* – which support the structure

above and *metopes* (broad panels usually carved with figurative scenes).

6 Pediments
Pediments are the triangular gables above the entablature on a temple's short sides, usually decorated with polychrome terracotta figures, reliefs or freestanding sculptures.

7 Roof
Roofs were made of wooden beams and terracotta tiles with polychrome decorations such as gargoyles cast into the shapes of animals' heads which functioned as water spouts.

8 Colour
Sculpted pieces and architectural elements, particularly the parts of the entablature and the pediment, were always painted in bright colours – most typically in red, blue, white or yellow.

9 Cella
Each temple housed a sanctuary *(cella)* which was usually an enclosed room in the centre of the temple. Here the sacred image or statue of a god was kept.

10 Altar
A carved block of stone used for animal sacrifices was placed outside temples at the eastern end.

Entablature and column

All of the finds from Selinunte can now be seen in Palermo, apart from the Efebo which is now in Castelvetrano.

Top 10 Finds from Selinunte

1 Punishment of Acteon (470 BC)
2 Efebo (bronze statue 470 BC)
3 Zeus and Hera (470 BC)
4 Perseus and the Gorgon (c.560–550 BC)
5 Statue of a Kore (6th century BC)
6 Tumminia Wheat
7 Europa and the Bull (6th century BC)
8 Corinthian Oinochoe (6th century BC)
9 Attic Lekane (6th century BC)
10 Bronze Zeus (6th century BC)

The Rise and Fall of Selinus

The 80,000 inhabitants of Selinus, named for the abundant wild celery (selinon) which still grows in the area, enjoyed prosperity and power with a sprawling urban complex, impressive temple compounds, their own mint and extensive agricultural holdings. Located on the edge of Greek territory, Selinus was forced to fight border wars with Segesta and was in constant danger from attack by their mighty Carthaginian allies. Although it gradually accepted some Carthaginian influence and even declared itself neutral in the Battle of Himera (480 BC) between the warring Carthaginians and Syracusan Greeks, it preferred to remain a Greek ally. Selinus lost that right in 409 BC when Hannibal and his forces sacked the town, forcing all inhabitants to abandon the residential sector. From then until its demise Selinus was restricted to the re-fortified Acropolis and remained under Punic control. Selinus was finally abandoned in 250 BC when Carthage, fighting Rome during the First Punic Wars, moved all residents to its stronghold at Lilybaeum (modern-day Marsala). A small community was located at Selinus during the Christian era, but it too was eventually abandoned and all knowledge of the town, even its name, was lost until archaeologists uncovered it in the 19th century.

Rediscovering Selinunte

Archaeological excavations, begun in the 1820s, continue today. In the ruins of the many temples, various architectural elements survive *(left)*, illustrating the one-time might of the city.

Hannibal sacking Selinus

Following pages: **Temple at Segesta (see p91)**

Left **The 1968 earthquake devastation** Right **Giuseppe Garibaldi**

Moments in History

1 Ducetius

In what was the last resistance effort against the Greeks, Ducetius unified his people, the Sicels of eastern Sicily, in 452 BC. He succeeded in fortifying positions and redistributing land until suffering final defeat at the hands of Syracuse.

2 Supremacy of Syracuse

The Syracusan tyrants Heiron I, Gelon, and Dionysus I assured the ascendancy of Greek Sicily, with Syracuse at the helm. The Greek colonies continued to fight among themselves, but united when necessary, including the defeat of the Carthaginians at Himera in 480 BC, calling a halt to 50 years of Carthaginian aggression.

3 Roman Rule

Rome's successful siege of Syracuse in 212 BC marked the end of Greek power on the island. After centuries of warfare, Roman rule brought peace. *Praetors* were sent to Sicily to govern, including the infamous

Roman invasion

Verres, later prosecuted by Cicero for his misdeeds. Verres, who looted everything from Sicilian wheat to works of art, was the first in a long line of foreign plunderers.

4 Arab Invasion

After three centuries of long-distance Byzantine rule, North African Moors invaded in 827 AD at Mazara del Vallo. Four years later they took Palermo, made it their capital and transformed it into the cosmopolitan city it remains today. They brought infrastructure to rural Sicily, improved irrigation and introduced new methods of agriculture and fishing.

5 Count Roger

Norman crusader Roger de Hautville (also known as Count Roger or Roger I) took Sicily at the end of the 11th century. He was the first of a century of Norman rulers who slowly changed Sicily from an eastern to a western society, albeit one with exotic flair *(see p9)*.

6 The Sicilian Vespers

Having been ruled for decades by the French Angevins, on Easter Monday 1282 an uprising began in Palermo. Using the excuse that a French soldier had insulted a woman, Sicilians killed every Frenchman on the island. Having successfully instigated revolt and done away with the unpopular foreign sovereign, Sicilians invited Peter of Aragón to become their king. Spanish domination lasted on the island for 500 years.

7 Giuseppe Garibaldi
Centuries of foreign domination, misrule and the feudal system meant wealth, power and land fell into the hands of the few. Popular revolts began in 1820, reached a head in 1848, and in May 1860 opened the way for the Italian socialist Garibaldi. With the aid of Sicilian Redshirts, Garibaldi took the island and convinced the peasant class to vote for Italian Unification.

8 Emigration
After Unification, however, Sicily found itself highly taxed and ignored as an outpost of a "foreign" government. Peasant farmers found themselves unable to feed their families and there was no means for improvement. Such poverty became the motivating factor for mass emigration to the Americas in the late 1800s and early 1900s.

9 Earthquakes
In 1908 an earthquake killed more than 70,000 people and levelled more than 90 per cent of Messina. The next quake, in 1968, left scores of villages destroyed in the Belice Valley. Thousands were housed in shelters for 15 years, waiting for the Italian government to resolve the problem.

10 Mafia Crackdown
More than 350 *mafiosi* were convicted during the late 1980s, as a result of which the judges Giovanni Falcone and Paolo Borsellino were murdered in 1992. "Boss of Bosses" Salvatore "Totò" Riina was finally convicted of arranging the murders.

Top 10 Mythological Figures

1 Aeneas
Aeneas fled Troy, found refuge on Sicily, and founded Erice and Segesta.

2 Demeter
All-important goddess of agriculture, the harvest and fertility, Demeter's cult was based at Enna.

3 Persephone
Demeter's daughter was abducted by Hades into the Underworld at Lake Pergusa.

4 Hephaestus (Vulcan)
The god of fire lived on Mount Etna forging his father Zeus's lightning bolts with the flames of the volcano.

5 Odysseus (Ulysses)
The Greek military leader wandered the Mediterranean for 10 years trying to get home. Many of his adventures took place on Sicily.

6 Polyphemus
The giant one-eyed Cyclops shepherd and cannibal held Odysseus hostage in his Mount Etna cave.

7 Aeolus
The King of the Winds and master of navigation lived on the Aeolian islands.

8 Arethusa
Chased by the river god Alpheus, Arethusa threw herself into the Ionian sea and sprung up at Syracuse, transformed into a fountain.

9 Acis
Murdered by the jealous Polyphemus, Acis was reincarnated into a river and gave his name to three towns on the Ionian coast.

10 Scylla
The hideous sea monster terrorized sailors passing the Straits of Messina.

Left **Museo Regionale Archeologico, Agrigento** Right **Museo Archeologico Regionale, Syracuse**

🔟 Museums

1 Museo Archeologico Regionale "Paolo Orsi", Syracuse

One of the most important archaeological museums in Sicily documents the ancient cultures and civilizations of both the city of Syracuse and eastern Sicily *(see pp20–21).*

2 Museo Regionale Archeologico, Agrigento

Extensive collections of archaeological finds from Agrigento and related cities reveal the Bronze Age through to Hellenization and the Roman age *(see pp28–9).*

3 Museo Regionale Agostino Pepoli, Trapani

The museum, housed in a 17th-century former monastery, is known for its extensive collection of decorative arts spanning from the 1600s to the 1800s, and includes coral pieces, jewellery and Nativity scene figurines. ◈ *Via Conte Agostino Pepoli 200, Trapani • Map B2 • Open 9am–1:30pm, 3–7pm daily • Adm*

4 Museo Regionale di Messina

This museum is home to architectural, sculptural and decorative fragments recovered from Messina's churches after the 1908 earthquake, as well as paintings and sculpture. Highlights include two works painted by Caravaggio during his stay in Messina in 1608–09: *The Raising of Lazarus* and *The Adoration of the Shepherds* with dramatically lit, monumental figures. ◈ *Viale della Libertà 465, Messina • Map H2 • Open 9am–2pm Mon–Sat, 4–7pm Tue, Thu & Sat, 9am–1pm Sun • Adm*

5 Museo Archeologico Regionale "Antonino Salinas", Palermo

Objects recovered from sites throughout western Sicily illustrate the development of art and culture from prehistoric eras to the Roman period. ◈ *Piazza Olivella, Palermo • Map L3 • Open 9am–2pm Mon, Wed, Thu & Sat, 9am–1pm, 3–6pm Tue & Fri, 9am–1pm Sun • Adm*

6 Galleria Regionale di Sicilia, Palazzo Abatellis, Palermo

The Catalan-Gothic palace was built at the end of the 15th century and is now home to the collections of the former National Museum. Paintings and sculpture by Sicilian masters span the 13th to 16th centuries, complemented by fine works by Italian and Flemish artists *(see p82).*

Palazzo Abatellis, Palermo

Museo delle Saline, Trapani

7 Museo delle Saline, Trapani

Housed in a restored windmill, exhibits here trace each fascinating stage of traditional salt-making, from filling the salt pans with sea water, to evaporation, recovering, storing, cleaning and grinding the salt *(see p94)*.

8 Aeolian Archaeological Museum, Lipari

Objects on display in this interesting museum range from obsidian tools of the Neolithic period to items acquired through foreign trade, such as Etruscan red-glazed ceramics. There are also beautiful vases and masks from Greece that have survived from Sicily's Greek occupation *(see p12)*.

9 Galleria Regionale del Palazzo Bellomo, Syracuse

The palace itself, built in 1234, is noteworthy for its medieval architecture with 15th-century Catalan additions. The collections trace the development of figurative art in southeast Sicily with medieval and Renaissance sculpture, Sicilian, Italian and Flemish paintings including works by Antonello and Caravaggio, and a collection of Sicilian decorative arts. ◎ *Via Capodieci 16, Syracuse • Map H5 • Open 9am–1:30pm Mon–Sat, 9am–12:30pm Sun • Adm*

10 Casa-Museo di Antonino Uccello, Palazzolo Acreide

The mission of Antonino Uccello was to preserve what he saw as the fast disappearing culture of peasant farmers. Every item used in the home, workroom, farm, for transportation, entertainment or devotion, was traditionally handmade. The result are elegantly crafted tools, illustrating a very personal and unique aspect of Sicilian history. ◎ *Via Machiavelli 19, Palazzolo Acreide • Map G5 • Open 9am–1pm, 3:30–7pm daily • Adm*

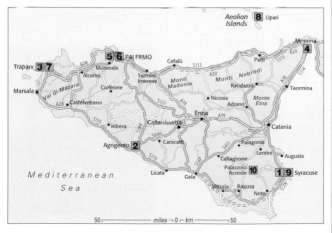

Left **Temple columns, Selinunte** Right **Mosaic, Villa Romana del Casale**

🔟 Ancient Sites

1 Taormina
Sited in a spectacular position on Monte Tauro, the 3rd-century BC Greek theatre at Taormina is the second largest in Sicily, but ranks first for the beauty of its backdrop. The view of Reggio di Calabria, the Ionian Sea and Mount Etna is broken only by the *scena* added later by the Romans – perhaps the marble-faced niches and columns were built because the view distracted spectators from any drama on the stage *(see pp14–15)*.

2 Syracuse
The Greeks founded a colony here in 733 BC and immediately began a programme of development and expansion that led Syracuse to become the most powerful city in the Mediterranean. Rich remains of defensive structures and sacred, social and residential areas are visible today within the modern city and in the surrounding area. A comprehensive archaeology museum makes sense of the varied ruins *(see pp18–21)*.

3 Villa Romana del Casale
The remains of a luxury hunting villa of a Roman official are the site of the best extant Roman mosaic cycle in the world. The rich figurative and decorative designs adorn the floors of the villa, which is situated in what was a forested area along the road from Catania to Agrigentum *(see pp24–5)*.

4 Agrigento
In the grounds of the famous Valle dei Templi lie wonderful Greek temples, and an important sanctuary to the goddesses Demeter and Persephone, the so-called Rock Sanctuary and the oldest at Agrigento. Now almost buried by the ugly mass of modern development is the medieval centre of the town, into which fascinating pieces of Greek structures were incorporated *(see pp26–9)*.

5 Selinunte
The evocative ruins of the residential and commercial sectors and monumental sacred structures are enclosed within the largest archaeological park in Europe. The site protects the ruins of eight massive temples, including one of the largest known temples of the ancient world, Temple C. There are also

Temple of Hera, Agrigento

visible remains of buildings left by the Phoenicians, Greeks, Carthaginians and a Byzantine settlement *(see pp30–33)*.

Segesta
6 This peaceful and beautiful site comprises the ruins of one of the most important cities of the Elimi, the Hellenized Sicani peoples, and one of the most perfect Doric temples ever constructed. The temple's purpose is unknown, adding further mystery to the already ethereal site – historians debate whether it was built to impress the Greeks in order to gain their military support, or whether it was to decorate a sacred site *(see p91)*.

Solunto
7 This village was under Carthaginian control along with Motya and Palermo until it was taken by the Romans around 250 BC. The grid pattern of the urban plan clearly remains and the paved streets are lined with residences and shops, some well preserved with traces of wall decoration, floor mosaics, steps, columns and cisterns. The latter were of supreme importance because Solunto's position on a promontory above the Tyrrhenian Sea did not offer any natural water sources *(see p94)*.

Morgantina
8 Morgantina was an important commercial centre along the trade route from the north coast of Sicily and the Aeolian Islands to the south, and extensive ancient remains have recently been excavated here. Deep in Sicani and Sicel territory, the city flourished during the Hellenistic and Roman periods, and most of the ruins date from that time *(see p110)*.

Motya

Motya
9 The island city in the lagoon between Marsala and Trapani was used from the 8th century BC by the Phoenicians as a base for controlling shipping routes in the eastern Mediterranean. It became a Carthaginian stronghold until its complete destruction by Syracuse in 397 BC. Today, the small island is covered with remains of that great city – walls with fortified gates and towers surround the entire perimeter and there is a man-made harbour within the walls. Ancient paved roads and sacred and residential areas can also be clearly seen *(see p92)*.

Giardini-Naxos
10 As the first Greek colony on Sicily and the site of the altar of Apollo Archegetes, protector god of all Greek settlements on the island, Naxos shouldn't be missed. Although the city was quickly surpassed by other colonies in wealth and power, it retained religious importance until it was destroyed by Syracuse in 403 BC. Its remaining inhabitants settled in nearby Taormina. The excavations of the ancient ruins can be seen on the headland *(see p100)*.

Left **Pasta** Right **Fico d'India cactus plants**

🔟 Vestiges of Invading Powers

1 Sicilian Dialect
It's not just an accent but a language of its own. Like Sicily itself, the dialect is a palimpsest created from foreign invasions and sounds like the exotic mix it is: a romance language with influences of Italian, Arabic, Latin, Greek, Lombard, Ligurian and English. Reflecting the fatalism of the populace, it has no future tense.

2 Pasta
Fresh pasta, made of regular wheat flour, was made in Italy as early as the Etruscan era. Dried pasta, which can be stored, was most likely invented by the Arabs using Sicily's *semola*, a hard durum wheat flour.

3 Place Names
Many place names are Italian versions of original Greek or Latin names. Erice was known as Monte San Giuliano until 1934 when Mussolini went on a name-changing spree and adopted an Italian version of its original Greek name, Eryx. Arabic names remain in abundance – look for names with the prefixes Calta, Gibil and Sala.

4 Urban Plans
Urban plans of modern towns often follow ancient street patterns. The area of narrow straight streets known as *la pettina* (the comb) in Syracuse is left over from the Greeks. The tiny, winding streets of Palermo's old neighbourhoods such as La Kalsa or the street plan of Castelvetrano come from Arab settlements. Cefalù's system of parallel streets leading down to the sea is Norman.

5 Fishing Techniques
Sicily's now famous fishing techniques were adapted from Arabic methods. Tuna fishermen still practise the *matanza* in the channel between Levanzo and Favignana, encouraging tuna through a system of nets until the final so-called "chamber of death" where they are brought close to the surface to be slaughtered. Fishermen work together chanting rhythmically to haul them aboard and to shore. Near Messina, swordfish are hunted from boats called *feluche*. The swordfish are spotted from the tall mast and harpooned from a long plank extending from the prow.

Matanza tuna fishermen

Sicilian lemon trees

6 Crops
The Spanish introduced tomatoes, potatoes, chocolate and the cactus *Fico d'India*; the Greeks introduced olive trees and grapevines; the Arabs brought citrus fruits, sugar cane, date palms, pistachios, flax, cotton and mulberries.

7 Fortified Towers
The Spanish protected Sicily's coastline with more than 100 defensive towers. Messages were passed from one to the other by fire signals.

8 Water Works
Greeks and Romans used aqueducts and water powered mills, while Arabs introduced land irrigation.

9 Erosion
The Romans began deforestation of the island to export timber and make way for wheat plantations. Sicily is now virtually treeless and the earth is easily washed away in heavy rains.

10 Latifondi
The system of single-owner wheat farms *(latifondi)* was codified by the Normans, so by the 1880s farmers had to compete for miniscule plots of land, resulting in mass poverty and eventually, mass immigration.

Top 10 Invaders

1 Greeks
The first Greek colony founded at Naxos in 734 BC displaced Sicel inhabitants.

2 Carthaginians
Carthage invaded repeatedly and many Punic War battles were fought on Sicily.

3 Romans
After years of warfare, Rome finally took Sicily after the fall of Syracuse in 212 BC.

4 Byzantines
In AD 535 Sicily became part of Justinian's Eastern Roman Empire.

5 Arabs
The Arab conquest of the island began in AD 827 and was complete only in AD 902 with the fall of Taormina.

6 Normans
After 30 years of crusades, Count Roger de Hautville took Sicily in 1091 *(see p36)*.

7 Spaniards
Peter of Aragón was crowned King of Sicily in 1282, beginning 440 years of Spanish domination.

8 Bourbons
Sicily was given to the House of Savoy in the 1713 Peace of Utrecht treaty, and swapped for Sardinia seven years later, thereby coming under Habsburg rule.

9 Italians
Garibaldi and his Red Shirts invaded at Marsala in 1860 starting the campaign that ended with the Unification of Italy.

10 Allied Forces
On 10 July 1943 Allied Forces under generals Patton and Montgomery landed at Gela and Pachino taking Sicily in 38 days.

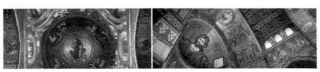

Left **La Martorana** Right **Monreale**

🔟 Places of Worship

1 Monreale
The monastery and Church of the Assumption were founded by William II in 1174. His tomb, along with the tombs of his family members including his father and mother, King William I and Queen Margaret, are located in the transept *(see pp10–11)*.

2 Cappella Palatina, Palermo
This masterpiece of Norman art celebrates both the Glory of God and successful Norman rule. Masses are said in the richly decorated chapel *(see p8)*.

3 San Domenico, Palermo
The "Pantheon" of Palermo is so-called because Sicily's most illustrious citizens are buried here. Among them are the physicist Stanislao Cannizzaro, the parliamentarian Ruggero Settimo, the painter Pietro Novelli, and other members of the nobility *(see p81)*.

4 Cathedral, Cefalù
In 1131, after several days on a stormy sea, Norman King Roger II landed safely at Cefalù and, giving thanks to God, endowed a bishopric and commissioned the cathedral now famous for its Byzantine mosaic decoration. In a piazza surrounded by tall palms, the church with its two typically Norman square bell towers is backed by Cefalù's dramatic rocky crag *(see p99)*. ◈ *Piazza Duomo • Map E2 • Open 7am–noon, 1:30–7pm daily • Free*

5 La Martorana, Palermo
The only original part of the exterior of this 1143 Norman masterpiece is its splendid bell tower, now minus its red dome. The original façade prompted an Arab traveller of 1184 to proclaim it the most magnificent building ever seen, so much so he hoped it would become a mosque. It never did *(see p81)*.

6 Santa Lucia, Syracuse
The Catholic Church often chose sites sacred to other cults on which to construct their places of worship, but this one is unique for being set within a previous site. Behind the Baroque façade, the structure of a Greek Temple to Athena has been adapted for use as a church. ◈ *Piazza Duomo • Map H5 • Open 7am–noon, 1:30–7pm daily • Free*

Cefalù Cathedral

San Nicola, Agrigento

7 San Nicola, Agrigento
The 13th-century church is located within the Valle dei Templi, and its façade incorporates Gothic motifs with ancient Roman columns. The interior was renovated in the early 1300s and the early 1400s. In a chapel on the right, there is an interesting Roman sarcophagus decorated with reliefs of Greek mythology *(see p24).* ✪ *Piazza Duomo • Map D4 • Open for weddings only • Free*

8 San Carlo al Corso, Noto
Dedicated to San Carlo Borromeo, the church of San Carlo is on the Corso and forms part of Noto's dramatic Baroque skyline. It is currently acting as the town's cathedral while the latter's dome is under repair *(see p23).* ✪ *Corso Vittorioema • Map G5 • Open 7am–noon, 1:30–7pm daily• Free*

9 San Giorgio, Ragusa
Ragusa's cathedral is built on a rise in a wide tree-lined piazza in the heart of the old town. The convex and undulating façade is typical of the architect Gagliardi, supporting a soaring central tower, bulging columns and swirly volutes. ✪ *Piazza S Giovanni • Map F5 • Open 8am–noon, 4–7pm • Free*

10 Other Faiths, Palermo
Given its long history of invasion *(see pp42–3),* Sicily has always been a cosmopolitan island, and nowhere more so than in its capital. Palermo is home to places of worship for a number for faiths, including a mosque – a clear remnant of its former Arab inhabitants.
✪ *Mosque: Piazza Gran Cancelliere 6; Opening times vary; Free • Evangelical Church: via Bara all'Olivella 11; Opening times vary; Free • Anglican Church: via Mariano Stabile 118b; Opening times vary; Free*

Left **Castello di Sperlinga** Right **Castello di Eurialo**

🔟 Castles

1 Castello di Eurialo
These 4th-century BC fortifications protected the western approach to mighty Greek Syracuse. Archimedes refined the structure adding a drawbridge, trenches and catapults to protect the keep. Descend into one of the defensive trenches where the tunnels *(gallerie)* give access to the keep (see p122).

2 Caccamo
Made of rough white stone, this 12th-century Norman castle dominates the village and valley below. Pass through the once impregnable walls, walk among ramparts, and visit the *Sala di Congiura* (Hall of the Conspiracy), where in 1160 the barons plotted to overthrow King William I. ✎ *Caccamo • Map D3 • Open 9:30am–noon, 1:30–6:30pm daily • Free*

3 Castello di Venere, Erice
This Norman castle is impressively sited on a sheer cliff face. The entrance through the tower is marked by the coat of arms of Charles V. Inside, the remains of Norman walls surround the ancient area sacred to Venus Erycina – stones from her temple were used to build the castle. There are also Phoenician and Roman ruins here. ✎ *Via Conte Pepoli • Map B2 • Open 8:30am–8:30pm daily • Free*

Castello di Venere

4 Castello di Lombardia, Enna
One of the largest castles in Sicily was built by Frederick II in 1233 on the highest point of the already towering village. Massive walls and defensive works remain in place, including six of what were once 20 towers. The octagonal Torre di Federico II is the only fully original part remaining. Climb the Torre Pisana for views of the city, the valley below and Mount Etna on the horizon. ✎ *Map E4 • Open 8am–8pm daily • Free*

5 Aci Castello
The castle is perched atop a black promontory, jutting out over the sea. Built by the Normans, it was later covered by lava flows in 1169. It was rebuilt by a traitor to the crown and thus partially destroyed by Frederick II of Aragón in 1297. A stairway scales the side of the fortifications giving access to the interior of the structure. The passages and chambers now hold the archaeological collection of the Museo Civico. ✎ *Map G4 • Open 9am–noon daily • Free*

Castello Ursino

6 Castello Ursino, Catania
Built around 1250, the once-moated castle has been used variously as a royal residence, the seat of parliament and a prison. It now houses the town's Museo Civico. ◎ Piazza Federico di Svevia • Map G4 • Open 9am–6pm Tue–Sun • Free

7 Castello Ventimiglia, Castelbuono
In 1316 the Ventimiglia family built their fortified family seat on top of a rocky outcrop in the heart of the Madonie mountains. The private rooms now house contemporary art and an ethnographic collection. ◎ Map E3 • Open 9am–1pm, 4–8pm Tue–Sun • Adm

8 Castello di Sperlinga
Sperlinga guarded the important royal Norman supply road linking Palermo with Catania. As the site of the only resistance to the Sicilian Vespers in 1282, a group of Angevins hid out here for more than a year. ◎ Via Castello • Map F3 • Open 9am–1pm, 4–8pm daily • Adm

9 Castello, Lipari
Above the harbour, Lipari's castle rock has been fortified for six millennia. The 12th-century Norman gate offers a passage through walls fortified with massive stones by the Greeks in the 4th century BC and again by the Spanish in 1556. ◎ Map G1 • Open 9am–1pm, 4–8pm Tue–Sun • Free

10 Castello di Donnafugata
Donnafugata is truly a hodgepodge of architectural styles. The Arabs first fortified the site around AD 1000; it then became a castle around 1300. In 1865 it was turned into a far grander building, and a Venetian Gothic loggia was added. ◎ Map F6 • Open 8:30am–1:30pm Tue–Fri, 9:30am–5:30pm Sat–Sun • Adm

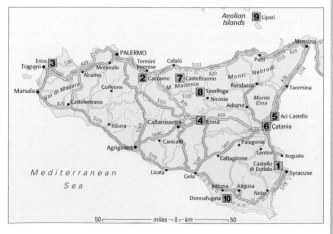

Left **Corleone** Right **Petralia Soprana**

🔟 Villages

1 Petralia Soprana

The highest village in the Madonie, at 1,147 m (3,760 ft) above sea level, medieval Petralia Soprana feels untouched by the modern world. Narrow alleyways are filled with the aroma of bakers making their traditional cinnamon biscuits, while the vistas of the rolling mountains below are breathtaking. ◈ *Map E3*

2 Scopello di Sopra

This small village of fishermen was almost inaccessible until recent years when the road was built from Castellammare. Now the village is experiencing something of a tourist boom, but retains the charm of a tiny fishing hamlet, and you'll still see an old mariner with nets stretched the length of the piazza, repairing the gaps with an enormous needle. ◈ *Map C2*

3 Poggioreale Vecchio and Poggioreale

In the heart of the Belice Valley, Poggioreale Vecchio (the old town) was founded in 1642 and managed to survive as a self-sufficient village until the earthquake of 1968 left it nothing more than a ghost town. Modern progress arrives slowly in the remote interior, and Poggioreale Vecchio looks much as it did in the 1800s. The people of old Poggioreale who were left homeless after the earthquake moved into a new government-sponsored town 15 years after the event. The new Poggioreale, a 1980s design by Paolo Portoghese, is full of flamboyant architecture, yet sadly filled with rather uninviting public spaces. ◈ *Map C3*

4 Cefalù

The ancient village was given new life in 1131 when Count Roger founded the cathedral here – its architecture and mosaic decoration make it one of Sicily's must-sees *(see p44)*. Although a constant tourist draw, the village has managed to keep some of its medieval character *(see p99)*.

5 Erice

Erice has managed to maintain much of its medieval charm. The buildings are all built of locally quarried white stone, adding to its storybook appearance. The steep streets

Cefalù

Erice

are also paved in characteristic patterns, the stones worn slick with time *(see p93)*.

6 Corleone
Made famous in the film *The Godfather (see p61)*, Corleone is the largest village in the area. A few 13th-century structures are visible in the centre. Ⓢ *Map C3*

7 Palazzo Adriano
In the heart of this fertile area, Palazzo Adriano is lofty and remote. In Piazza Umberto I are two main churches, the Catholic Santa Maria del Lume, and the Greek Orthodox Santa Maria Assunta, built by Albanian refugees in the 1400s. Palazzo Adriano gained fame in 1990 as the setting for the Academy Award-winning film *Cinema Paradiso (see p61)*. Ⓢ *Map D3*

8 Novara di Sicilia
This little mountain village is tucked away between the Peloritani and Nebrodi mountain ranges. The medieval site has a crumbling Arab castle and the 16th-century Chiesa Madrice with naïve wood carvings on the altar. Ⓢ *Map G2*

9 Palazzolo Acreide
Palazzolo Acreide is a lovely village with an impressive mix of sites – originally Greek, most of what you see today is Baroque. The churches are spectacular, particularly the tiny Church of the Annunciation with its twisting columns. Ⓢ *Map G5*

10 Scicli
Rebuilt after the earthquake of 1693, Scicli combines open, tree-lined piazzas, swirling Baroque façades and older structures with terracotta tiled roofs. Ⓢ *Map F6*

Left **Gulfo di Castellammare** Right **Selinunte beach**

🔟 Beaches

1 Selinunte
A large sandy beach stretches to the east of the port and just below the temples *(see pp30–33)*. Bathing establishments offer beach chairs, watersports equipment, restaurants and bars. It tends to be crowded with students showing off their skimpy suits and tans, but through the small pine wood to the west you'll find an open beach for families. ◎ *Map B4*

2 Gulfo di Castellammare
The beaches west of Castellammare are prettier and less populated than those to the east. There are plenty of gorgeous coves with clear water – most spectacular are those with pebble beaches in Lo Zingaro *(see p91)* and at Scopello Tonnara, with its rock towers and old boat ramp for sunbathing. ◎ *Map C2*

3 Eraclea Minoa
Below the ruins of the Greek city *(see p110)* a little seaside village comes to life in summer. The sandy beach is long, wide and open, and buffered by pine woods. At either end are two bars providing beach chairs and snacks. ◎ *Map C4*

4 Mazzarò & Giardini Naxos
The water at the two resorts below Taormina is a calm, brilliant blue. The cable car from Taormina descends to Mazzarò, a developed resort area with two pebble beaches lined with well-equipped bathing establishments, coves for exploring and the popular island of Isola Bella *(see p15)*. Giardini Naxos is a fully fledged town with a port and long stretches of beach lined with hotels *(see p100)*.

5 Mondello
This is Palermo's backyard. It is crowded with seaside villas of Palermo's aristocracy and locals of all walks of life taking advantage of the beach, bars, *gelaterie*, restaurants and clubs. For swimming, nature and tranquillity this may not be the best beach in Sicily, but it's high on the list for those who want to participate in the scene. ◎ *Map D2*

6 Pollara, Salina
The black beach here is a luxurious stretch of open, isolated, sparkling sands with a dramatic lava cliff backdrop. The view out to the sea is just as dramatic, with a craggy *faraglione* (rock tower) poking up out of the

View of Mazzarò

For tips on water safety See p137

Mondello

dark sea. As there is little development here, bring food and drink from town or get supplies from the vendor and his friends at the booth set up in the church piazza *(see p13)*.

7 Scoglitti & Donnalucata

The sandy beaches along this southeast stretch of coast are long and wide and splashed with green-blue surf. There is no tourist development to speak of, beyond small fishing villages such as Scoglitti and Donnalucata with their nice markets and good restaurants, and little seaside villages that come to life in summer, such as Marina di Ragusa. ✆ *Map F6*

8 Lampedusa

The tiny islet Isola dei Conigli, off Lampedusa, and the bay in between have been set apart as a nature reserve for sea turtles who lay their eggs on the beach. The water is clean and shallow in the bay and the sands are white but there are no facilities so bring your own supplies. ✆ *Map B6*

9 Aci Castello

Here clear, blue water laps onto the black lava rocks just below the castle *(see p46)*. Descend to the left where a water polo court is set up in summer, or to the right to a wooden deck for sunbathing and diving. ✆ *Map G4*

10 Vendicari

A spectacular nature reserve with sandy beaches set around a 15th-century Aragonese tower. The pristine coast here offers a peaceful, natural experience. The park is covered with Mediterranean maquis, and its wetland habitat provides a resting stop for birds migrating to and from Africa. ✆ *Map G6*

Left **Boating** Right **Sunbathing on a water dinghy**

Outdoor Activities

1 The Passeggiata
Walking up and down a city or village's main street is Sicily's supreme activity, allowing for socializing, doing business and people-watching *(see p69)*.

2 Swimming
The unspoiled, clear water off Sicily and the offshore islands is spectacular, and also great for snorkelling and scuba-diving. The shoreline varies from sandy to pebble beaches, private coves, grottoes and rock formations. Lifeguards are rarely on duty, so swim at your own risk *(see p137)*.

3 Skiing, Mount Etna
The depth of snow depends upon underground lava flows that affect surface temperatures, but there's enough of a base for winter-time skiing at least on the northern slopes. Pick a base at Zafferana Etnea, Nicolosi or Linguaglossa where ski rentals, a ski school and lifts are available *(see pp16–17)*.

The Passeggiata

4 Mount Etna Sunset and Sunrise
Enjoy amazing sunsets and sunrises from high on the slopes of Mount Etna. The early morning sunrise offers spectacular colours and excellent views as the sky is often clear at this time. Or stay below and take advantage of the sunrise to fully appreciate the magnitude of the volcano whose shadow stretches far to the west.

5 Hiking
Find great hikes all over the island, whether you're looking for a strenuous climb up a volcano, a long walk through the green hills of the interior or an exciting hike on trails clinging to the cliffs above the blue sea. Most nature reserves are *orientata* (orientated), meaning that they have marked trails that are usually graded for difficulty. Try Mount Etna, Stromboli or Vulcano, or the gorges of the southeast. Lo Zingaro has a good selection of trails ranging in difficulty, as do the parks of the Nebrodi and Madonie mountain ranges *(see p101)*.

6 Fishing, Favignana
You can't join in the traditional *matanza* fishing ritual, although you can watch it in progress if you happen to be there when the tuna are running *(see p42)*. You can also rent a boat with a local captain for a day's fishing.

Following the October 2002 eruption some ski runs on Mount Etna will have to be replaced. Telephone ahead for details.

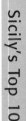

Sicily's Top 10

Horse riding, Madonie Mountains

7 Horse Riding

Nature reserves such as Mount Etna, the Madonie and Nebrodi mountain ranges and Lo Zingaro are populated with small farms that rent horses. Ask at the nearest base hotel or check park literature for *equiturismo* and *maneggio* (stables).

8 Cycling

All but the most serious cyclists may have a rough time on the steep terrain and on roads populated by Sicilian drivers who are not on the lookout for bikes. Cycling is a great way to sightsee in towns, however, and many offer free bike rentals through tourist offices. Renting a bicycle on the offshore islands is a convenient way to get around.

9 Boating

Sail your own, arriving at one of Sicily's many ports *(see p130)*, or rent a boat and a captain for an insider's tour of hidden coves.

10 Watersports

Diving and snorkelling are available with trained guides through diving centres in Scopello and the Aeolian Islands, or snorkel on your own, taking advantage of the marine life along Sicily's shores. Beaches in more touristy areas rent pedal boats and windsurfing boards.

Top 10 Sicilian Flora and Fauna

1 Sea Turtles
Rare sea turtles bury their eggs in the sands of the Belice Estuary and the Pelagie Islands.

2 Sanfratellano Horse
A species indigenous to the Nebrodi, descendant of the ancient *Equus sicanus*.

3 Birds of Prey
Golden eagles, peregrine falcons and owls hunt in the island's nature reserves.

4 Cactus
The *Fico d'India*, or prickly pear, is omnipresent as it thrives in Sicily's arid climate.

5 Dwarf Palm
The tiny palm flourishes in the northwest; its fronds are used by craftsmen for weaving baskets and brooms.

6 Fennel
Bright yellow, fluffy green or tall and crispy brown, depending upon the season, it covers hillsides and springs up along the side of roads.

7 Agave
The low-growing aloe-like plant with curling spiky leaves shoots out a central stalk that can reach up to 12 m (40 ft).

8 Flowering Vines
Growing out of control and perfuming the countryside are jasmine, bougainvillea, honeysuckle and morning glory.

9 Thistle
The hearty, spiky plant pops up along roadsides and in fields with its bright purple flowers – not to be confused with cultivated artichokes.

10 Forests
The few remains of once prevalent pine, oak, cork-oak and beech forests are now carefully protected.

For specialist activity holidays in Sicily **See p131**

Left **Puppets** Right **Museo delle Saline**

🔟 Children's Attractions

1 Puppet Theatres
Puppet theatres offer rip-roaring, gory re-enactments of the Norman crusader sword fights, lively music, and encourage the audience to root for a favourite crusader. The puppets "speak" in Italian, or Sicilian dialect, but an English-language written account of the story is usually provided by the theatre. In any event, it's easy enough to follow the action without understanding every word *(see pp64–5)*.

2 Castles
All of Sicily's invaders needed to defend their position, so they built fortified castles along the coastline and on high points inland to guard the roads and towns. Sicily's countless castles are rich in history and offer plenty of good romping around the ramparts, searching for secret passageways, dungeons, trapdoors, tiny spy windows and hidden places from which the occupants would pour boiling oil down onto the enemy *(see pp46–7)*.

Children at the beach

3 Beaches
The bathing establishments found on most beaches offer chair and umbrella rentals, and many rent out pedal boats and watersports equipment such as windsurfing boards. Kids love snorkelling in Sicily's clear waters, where an entire eco-system of fish and shellfish live near the shoreline. Masks, flippers, floating boards and other snorkelling equipment can be purchased from even the smallest of shops in seaside villages *(see pp50–51)*.

4 Museo delle Saline
Just south of Trapani, the small museum of salt is located inside a restored windmill. Its fascinating exhibits show how the windmill transfers water from pool to pool and grinds the harvested salt. Work in the salt pans themselves is on-going and you can see each stage that goes into transforming sea water to table salt *(see p94)*.

5 Grotesques
Baroque architecture made good use of hideous monsters, goofy Turks (the long-standing Sicilian enemy), animals and chubby flying angels on horseback as supports for balconies or general decoration on the exteriors of buildings. Usually located under balconies, they also lurk above windows and doors, on corners, along the cornices and even on city gates.

Aquarium, Syracuse

6 Aquarium, Syracuse

The Syracuse *Acquario* offers a close look at marine life in the Mediterranean, housed in 40 different tanks. Additional sections are dedicated to fresh-water and tropical habitats. Located at the Fonte Aretusa on the island of Ortygia, entry is from the marina below. ◎ *Ortygia* • *Map H5* • *Open 10am–10pm Mon–Sat* • *Adm*

7 Motya

The archaeological park on the island of Motya starts and ends with a short boat ride across the lagoon (less than 10 minutes each way). The park itself is wide open, and offers excellent examples to inquisitive kids of how the Phoenicians and then the Carthaginians lived and fortified their villages. In addition to Motya, all of Sicily's archaeological parks offer space to run around and usually ruins to climb about on *(see p92)*.

8 Pizzerie

Sicily is full of *pizzerie (see pp76–7)*, many of which are specifically geared towards families. Often they are outfitted with playgrounds and video games. At such venues, the traditional pizza toppings often give way to children's idiosyncracies – don't be surprised to find the dough base topped with hotdogs and French fries, for example. Kids particularly enjoy Boffo's Castle, the Selinunte *pizzeria* built to resemble a fanciful Norman castle. ◎ *Ristorante Boffo's Castle (road to Castelvetrano), Contrada Martelluzzi, 101 • Map B3 • 0924 46860 • €*

9 Swimming Pools

Swimming pools are available at holiday villages *(see p146)* and some other hotels, but don't expect lifeguards to be on duty, or if they are, to be particularly attentive. Seaside villages often have a nearby water park, such as Acquasplash near Selinunte, with supervised wave pools, slides, a *pizzeria* or snack bar, as well as other diversions. ◎ *Acquasplash, via Tonnara 17, Tre Fontane • Map B4 • Open 9am–6pm Mon–Fri • Adm*

10 Nature Reserves

Sicily's nature reserves are good places to spot wildlife, climb about, picnic and go swimming. Hiking trails are graded for various levels of expertise. Mount Etna *(see pp16–17)* is probably the most fascinating for kids and adults alike – the volcano is always at least smoking, if not throwing red sparks into the air. Guides give a lively account of lava flowing underfoot and the gift shops screen spectacular video footage from past eruptions.

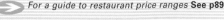
Traditional Sicilian pizza

→ *For a guide to restaurant price ranges See p89*

Left **Carnevale, Sciacca** Right **Santa Rosalia celebrations, Palermo**

🔟 Festivals

1 Santa Lucia, Syracuse
A procession of a silver statue of Syracuse's patron saint travels from the Duomo to the Chiesa di Santa Lucia, built on the spot where she was martyred in AD 304. As the protectress of eyesight, the faithful attach votive eyes made from silver, bronze or wax to her image. ◈ *13 Dec*

2 San Paolo and San Sebastiano, Palazzolo Acreide
Rivals for centuries, the land-owners and farmers loyal to San Paolo and the artisans and merchants loyal to San Sebastiano try to out-celebrate each other. Huge statues of the saints make an entrance from the church into the piazza where they are met with brightly coloured streamers, then journey through the village. Worshippers process barefoot well into the night. ◈ *San Paolo: 29 Jun; San Sebastiano: 10 Aug*

Santa Lucia statue, Syracuse

3 Santa Rosalia, Palermo
Rosalia was the daughter of a nobleman but chose a hermitic life in a cave on Monte Pellegrino. The discovery of her relics "saved" Palermo from the plague in 1624. For six days, her relics, atop an ornate *vara* (float), are paraded around the streets of the city. ◈ *9–14 Jul*

4 San Giuseppe, Belice Valley
St Joseph's Day is celebrated fervently in the west, especially in villages such as Salemi and Poggioreale. Altars are constructed in homes, schools and public spaces, piled high with ornate breads and traditional foods – but no meat, out of respect for St Joseph's poverty. ◈ *18–19 Mar*

5 Venerdì Santo, Noto
The Holy Thorn is processed through the streets accompanied by the black-veiled Grieving Madonna. The solemn procession is accompanied by a drum and a trumpet, periodically letting out a mournful blast. ◈ *Good Fri*

6 Festival of the Assumption, Randazzo
One of the most spectacular floats of all the Sicilian festivals is paraded from Piazza di Santa Maria through the narrow streets of the village to Piazza Loreto. The tall float carries young local boys dressed up as angels, saints, Jesus and the Madonna. ◈ *15 Aug*

Sant'Agata festival, Catania

7 Sant'Agata, Catania

One of the earliest saints, Agata was martyred in Catania's Piazza Stesicoro. The bejewelled reliquary bust of the saint is paraded around town followed by fanciful golden "candlesticks" so large that each one is hauled on the backs of 10 men. Balconies are draped in fabrics, flags fly, candles burn, and fireworks thunder at dawn. ✎ 5 Feb

8 Good Friday, Trapani

A procession of 20 huge scenes of Christ's Passion, decorated with flowers, is accompanied by bands playing funeral dirges.

9 Easter Sunday, Castelvetrano

Crowds gather in Castelvetrano to see the statue of Christ enter from one end of the piazza, while the Madonna enters from the other. To a dramatic drumbeat, they move toward one another and come together in an embrace. ✎ Easter Sun

10 Carnivale, Sciacca, Taormina, Acireale

The historic streets of these towns are packed with revellers for parades, parties and competitions. *Papier mâché* floats satirize current events or figures of popular culture. ✎ Feb

Top 10 Food Festivals

1 Mostra dei Formaggi della Valle del Belice e Sagra della Ricotta, Poggioreale

Watch ricotta made in traditional and modern methods. ✎ Last weekend May.

2 Sagra della Pesca, Bivona

A peach festival, with local food and popular music. ✎ 2nd or 3rd weekend Aug

3 Cous Cous Fest, San Vito lo Capo

Chefs compete in a cous cous contest, with tastings. ✎ Last week Sep

4 Sagra della Ciliegia, Chiusa Sclafani

Cherry festival, with traditional folk music. ✎ 1st or 2nd Sun Jun

5 Sagra del Pesce Azzuro, Selinunte

A procession of the Madonna of the Fishermen and a sardine feast. ✎ Late Aug

6 Fiera della Gastronomia dell'Etna

Throughout Zafferana Etnea, a fair of local wine, chestnuts, cheese, honey and mushrooms. ✎ Every Sun Oct

7 Sagra del Mare, Sciacca

Fish festival at the port. ✎ 27–29 Jun

8 Sagra del Carciofo, Cerda

Artichoke festival, and music in the main piazza. ✎ 25 Apr

9 Sagra del Carrubo, Frigintini

A tasting of pasta and carob biscuits. ✎ Late Sep–early Oct

10 Sagra delle Scaccie, Acate

Local treats, including carob, breads, olive oil, wine and cheese. ✎ 2nd week Sep

Left **Harvesting olives for olive oil** Right **Grapes for wine-making**

TOP 10 Customs and Traditions

1 Hand Gestures
A Grand Tour author reported that Sicilians had been using hand gestures since the Greek invasion as a way of furthering resistance against foreign rule. Some of the common gestures you see mean: "She's pretty", "This tastes great", "Let's go", "I couldn't care less", "Do you want to stop for a coffee?", "Be careful", "That's not such a good idea" and "His wife is cheating on him".

2 Proverbs
No good Sicilian is ever without a witty quip spoken in dialect. Examples include: *Cu' avi 'nna bona vigna, avi pani, vinu e ligna* (he who owns a good vineyard has bread, wine and wood); *Cu nun 'sapi l'arti, chiudi putia* (he who does not know his craft, closes his shop); *Soggira e nora calaru di n'celu sciarriannus* (mothers-in-law and daughters-in-law were sent from heaven and started fighting before they hit the ground); and *La soggira voli bene a la nora comu n'rizzu n'pettu* (mothers-in-law love their daughters-in-law like a sea urchin in bed).

3 I Morti
The feast of All Souls on 2 November is celebrated to the hilt. Families visit the cemetery where tombs have been rigorously tidied up and adorned with fresh flowers for the glory of the dead and for approval of family members and anyone else casting a judgmental eye. Relatives from the other world leave gifts for children, such as toys, *frutta martorana* (fake fruits crafted of almond paste) and *pupi di cena*, garishly coloured sugar dolls.

4 Festivals
Festivals for patron saints once offered the only chance for a holiday, socializing and entertainment. Celebrated in spring giving farmers a chance to rest after the planting and to pray for a successful harvest, the *festa* was the one day everyone came in from the fields for religious processions, games, horse races, music and fireworks. Even the *gelato* salesman and puppet theatre came to town. The same festivals are still celebrated as a chance to dress up and get together *(see pp56–7)*.

Sicilian festival

5 Legends

King Roger's 12th-century French court poets told stories of Charlemagne and the paladins and the King Arthur cycle which once included Sicily in its milieu: Morgan Le Fay took wounded King Arthur to recover in a cave on Mount Etna. The paladins survive today as puppet theatre heroes *(see pp64–5)* and Morgan Le Fay retained her presence in Sicily as *Fata Morgana*, who appears as a mirage over the Straits of Messina.

6 La Befana

This craggy old woman who declined an invitation to join the Three Kings bringing gifts to Christ in the manger regretted her decision, set out on her own, and has been travelling the earth with a sackful of gifts ever since. At Epiphany (6 January) she fills children's socks with presents if they've been good or with coal if they've been bad.

7 Olive Oil

On 11 November St Martin's Day, families celebrate their new, thick, spicy, green olive oil by sampling it on *i muffuletti*, round sandwich loaves baked with fennel seeds and dressed with salt and oil. If they don't have their own olive trees, families obtain a year's supply of olive oil from a relative or another trusted source, making sure to have a full *giara*, a waist-high terracotta storage jar.

8 Wine

A glass of new wine accompanies *i muffuletti* on St Martin's Day – usually strong, amber-coloured wine retrieved from the *botte* (barrel). Many families have at least enough grapevines for a yearly *botte* of wine, keeping it in the cellar if there is one, and if not, in the garage or anywhere else they can find as a cool spot.

9 Water Usage

Out of habit and necessity, Sicilians fiercely conserve water. Indoor plumbing did not reach the rural interior until the 1950s. Even where there is and has been plumbing, there is often no water due to poor or non-existent pipes. Bowls are often placed under spouts and spigots to catch an errant drop, and water is recycled – water from boiling pasta, for example, is given to pets instead of spilled down the drain.

Sicilian fisherman and his catch

10 Artigianal Fishing

Although fishing is big business, there are still artigianal fleets fishing Sicily's waters using *cannizzi*, hand-made cane switches called fish-aggregating devices. Hand-made lobster pots and colourful nets are also used. Find artisans making *cannizzi* and pots and chat with fishermen who sell their own catch at local markets, or watch as they repair their nets in the afternoons.

Left **Giuseppe Tomasi di Lampedusa** Right **Luigi Pirandello**

Artists, Writers and Composers

1 Aeschylus

The "Father of Greek tragedy" (525–456 BC) was born near Athens but made extended visits to Sicily. Only seven of around 500 plays have survived the centuries, among them *Agamemnon*, *Oedipus* and *Prometheus Bound*. Many of his plays were premiered in Syracuse's theatre *(see p18)*, where they are still performed.

2 Antonello da Messina

Messina-born Antonello (c.1430–79) is one of the masters of Italian Renaissance art, known for his exacting detail, intriguing portraits and the luminous quality of his paintings. He achieved the latter through his skilful use of oil paints, a technique he learned from Flemish masters. Italian Renaissance artists adopted oils in his wake and it became the

Antonello da Messina

standard medium for the world's greatest masterpieces. The few Antonello works that remain in Sicily are in museums in Palermo, Messina, Syracuse and Cefalù.

3 The Gagini Family

The Gagini family set the style for architecture and sculpture in Sicily during the 15th and 16th centuries. Inspired by elements of northern and central Italian art, the Gagini combined Renaissance and Gothic forms to create uniquely Sicilian pieces. Domenico (d.1492) was influenced by Ghiberti and Brunelleschi, and opened a workshop in Palermo. His son Antonello (1478–1536) produced delicately modelled, classic sculpture in the tradition of 15th-century Florence, in materials from marble to stucco.

4 Giacomo Serpotta

The Palermo-born artist (1656–1732) decorated Baroque interiors, creating an aesthetic transition between architecture and paintings by covering all available space with figures and scenes modelled in stucco.

5 Vincenzo Bellini

The composer (1801–35) was born in Catania, trained in Naples and is buried in Catania's cathedral. His successful early works led to commissions for La Scala in Milan. *The Sleepwalker* and *Norma* are among his most successful operas.

Scene from *Norma* by Vincenzo Bellini

6 Luigi Pirandello

Born at Caos near Agrigento, Pirandello (1867–1936) is known as the founder of 20th-century drama. His best-known work is the play *Six Characters in Search of an Author* (1921).

7 Giuseppe Tomasi di Lampedusa

Lampedusa (1896–1957) is the author of *Il Gattopardo (The Leopard)*, the classic portrait of Sicilian aristocracy pre- and post-Unification. It was based on the life of his great-grandfather and published posthumously.

8 Salvatore Quasimodo

Born in Modica, Quasimodo (1901–68) wrote anti-Fascist works in a political climate that made it necessary to disguise his message. He was awarded the Nobel Prize in 1959.

9 Renato Guttuso

From Bagheria, Guttuso (1912–87) painted energetic canvases that spoke out against the Mafia and Fascism and illustrated Sicilian peasant life.

10 Leonardo Sciascia

Sciascia (1921–89) was a political essayist and novelist. Works such as *The Wine Dark Sea* give insight into the complicated world of Sicilian thinking and Mafia culture.

Top 10 Films Set in Sicily

1 La Terra Trema

Visconti's 1948 adaptation of Verga's *I Malavoglia*, the story of a fisherman's failed dream of independence.

2 Divorzio all'Italiana

Pietro Germi's 1961 comedy has Marcello Mastroianni as a Sicilian aristocrat seeking a divorce when divorce in Italy was not legal.

3 A Ciascuno il Suo

Adapted from a Sciascia novel, a look into the Mafia and life in 1960s Sicily, directed by Elio Petri in 1967.

4 Il Gattopardo

Luchino Visconti's 1968 film version of Lampedusa's novel stars Burt Lancaster.

5 Giorno della Civetta

A 1968 Mafia murder thriller adapted from Sciascia's novel *The Day of the Owl*.

6 The Godfather

Francis Ford Coppola's 1972 Mafia classic with Marlon Brando as the Don Corleone.

7 Cento Giorni a Palermo

Giuseppe Ferrara's 1983 film documents the story of policeman Carlo Alberto Della Chiesa, murdered by the Mafia after just 100 days on the job.

8 Kaos

A 1984 film adaptation of four Pirandello stories.

9 Cinema Paradiso

Giuseppe Tornatore's 1989 Academy Award-winning film takes a romantic look at growing up in a remote village.

10 Il Postino

The life of a Sicilian fisherman-cum-postman is turned around through his friendship with the Chilean poet, Pablo Neruda (1994).

Left **Teatro Massimo, Palermo** Right **Teatro Politeama Garibaldi, Palermo**

🔟 Performing Arts Venues

1 Teatro Antica di Segesta

At one of the most spectacularly sited theatres of the ancient world, experience Greek tragedy and comedy, modern dramatic productions, orchestral music with the Sicilian Symphonic Orchestra and the Orchestra of Teatro Massimo, plus world music from various guest artists. The theatre runs a full season with performances staged nightly from early July through to the end of August.
🔖 *Archaeological site • Map C3*

2 Greek Theatre, Syracuse

Classical theatre is staged during the spring of even numbered years in Syracuse's ancient theatre, with daily performances from mid-May through to the end of June. The largest and one of the oldest theatres of ancient Sicily is for the most part intact and accepts modern stage sets and seating. Don't miss one of Aeschylus's tragedies in the theatre where they premiered thousands of years ago *(see p18)*.

3 Archaeological Park, Selinunte

During the month of August performances of Greek drama, classical and modern dance, and music are staged among the ruins in Selinunte's archaeo-logical park. Pick a spot among the temples and have a picnic under the stars. Performances start at 9pm *(see pp30–31)*.

4 Teatro Massimo & Teatro Politeama Garibaldi, Palermo

The Teatro Massimo was built in the 1880s as a grand symbol of post-Unification Sicily by Neo-Classical architects Giovanni Battista Basile and his son Ernesto. Although noted for its grandeur and for superb acoustics, the theatre was allowed to fall into decline and was closed for almost a quarter century. After a massive renovation effort, the doors were reopened in 1997, and once again it is Palermo's premier venue for classical music, ballet and opera. Ballet as well as symphonic concerts can also be enjoyed at the city's Teatro Politeama, which roughly marks the border between old and modern Palermo *(see p88)*.

5 Il Teatro Massimo Bellini, Catania

Catania's great opera house, named after the much loved native-born composer Vincenzo Bellini *(see p60)*, lies in the heart

Il Teatro Massimo Bellini, Catania

You can purchase tickets for performances at Syracuse's ancient theatre via Ticket One at www.ticketone.it

of the city. The grand theatre, influenced by the Paris Opéra, opened its doors in 1890 with a performance of Bellini's masterpiece *Norma* – the opera was so popular Sicilians even named a pasta dish after it. The season of opera and concerts, including chamber music, and ballet performances by the theatre ballet company runs from October through to June. ✆ *Via Perrota 12, Catania • Map G4*

Luigi Pirandello statue, Teatro Luigi Pirandello

Lo Spasimo, Palermo
6 The open nave of Santa Maria dello Spasimo alla Kalsa, a former church, is a romantic venue for performances and film. Music can be heard from the upper outdoor terrace as well, while artworks are on display in the covered exhibition space. It is an innovative and resourceful use for one of Palermo's damaged historic buildings and one of the first venues to start the revival of the Kalsa neighbourhood *(see p88)*.

Teatro Luigi Pirandello, Agrigento
7 The ornate civic theatre of Agrigento was inaugurated in 1880 as the third largest theatre in Sicily after the Teatro Massimo in Palermo and the Teatro Bellini in Catania. The venue was dedicated to the Agrigento native playwright Luigi Pirandello on the 10th anniversary of his death in 1945 *(see p61)*. The season runs from November through May with performances of modern theatre and dance, as well as, of course, productions of works by the great playwright himself,

such as *Six Characters in Search of an Author*.
✆ *Piazza Luigi Pirandello, Agrigento • Map D4*

Il Piccolo Teatro dei Pupi Fratelli Mauceri, Syracuse
8 Puppeteer Alfredo Mauceri directs traditional puppet performances in the Catania style *(see p64)* as well as plays of the lives of the saints, and the Mauceri family's own productions such as *Alpheus*, based on the myth of Alpheus and Arethusa. You can also watch puppets being made and antique puppets being restored in the family workshop down the street. ✆ *Via della Giudecca 17, Syracuse • Map H5*

Vincenzo Argento Opera dei Pupi, Palermo
9 For four generations the Argento family have been producing puppet shows based on Ariosto's *Orlando Furioso*. Today Vincenzo Argento and his three children run the theatre, making their own puppets and painting their own scenery in the theatre workshop near Palermo's cathedral. ✆ *Palazzo Asmundo, via Pietro Novelli 1, Palermo • Map K5*

Il Teatro dell'Opera dei Pupi, Palermo
10 A traditional puppet theatre staged by Palermitan master puppeteer Girolamo Cuticchio. See popular shows of Charlemagne and his paladins *(see pp64–5)*, plus stories of Sicilian saints, brigands and even *Don Quixote* and *Snow White and the Seven Dwarfs*. There is also a Cuticchio theatre in Cefalù. ✆ *Via dei Benedettini 9, Palermo • Map J6*

Left & Right **Puppets, Museo Internazionale delle Marionette Antonio Pasqualino, Palermo**

Puppet Traditions and Museums

1 Origins
There were puppeteers in ancient Syracuse, but the *opera dei pupi* as we know it today really became popular in the 1800s. Puppet theatres provided nightly entertainment for thousands of Sicilians – Palermo had more than 25 theatres where full houses would watch the good guys fight the bad guys in stories of adventure and romance, chivalry and treachery. Travelling puppet theatres drew huge crowds in smaller villages.

2 Catanese School
Puppets of the Catania tradition are almost 1.5 m (5 ft) tall. Puppeteers manoeuvre the heavy puppets via a metal pole attached to the heads, moving their limbs with strings. The puppets' joints are fixed and the swords of the paladins are constantly drawn. They inhabit a narrow stage with a long horizontal backdrop and are sometimes accompanied in the action by live actors.

Palermitan puppet

3 Palermitan School
Palermitan puppets are around 1 m (3 ft) tall. They are entirely manipulated by strings, have movable joints and can raise their face guards and draw their swords at will. Because they are lighter, they are more easily manipulated and their sword fights are much more lively. The stage of the Palermo-style theatre is a deeply recessed space with room for many characters and backed by elaborately decorated scenery.

4 Stories
The most traditional subjects are derived from the epic poems of the Carolingian cycle, retold by Ludovico Ariosto in his 1516 *Orlando Furioso*. Holy Roman Emperor Charlemagne and his paladins battle for Christianity against the Saracens and Turks and raucous sword fights abound. Other productions relate the lives of the saints, stories of bandits, Shakespearian themes and local farces.

5 The Good Guys
Holy Roman Emperor Charlemagne and his paladins are dressed in armour and skirts and brightly coloured silks. Orlando, mighty and loyal leader of the paladins, carries a shield with a cross. His cousin Rinaldo, a brave fighter with a weakness for the ladies, is identified by the lion on his shield, as is his long-haired sister Bradamante,

For places to see puppet theatre in action **See pp62–3**

another warrior. Angelica, the object of the two men's affections, can be cunning but is usually on their side.

6 The Bad Guys
Mostly evil Saracens and Turks, they wear baggy trousers and droopy moustaches and bear shields decorated with a crescent moon. Charlemagne's brother-in-law and arch-enemy Gano di Magonza often tries to overthrow the crown. Sorcerer Malagigi plays both sides, sometimes helping, sometimes hurting the paladins' cause.

7 Museo Internazionale delle Marionette Antonio Pasqualino, Palermo
The extensive collection includes examples of puppet traditions from all over the world. Among the puppets and scenery are examples of famous Sicilian *pupari* (puppeteers) representing the Palermo and Catania schools, complete with puppets, stages and sets. There is a theatre with performances staged by the Cuticchio family *(see p63)*. ⊗ *Via Butera 1, Palermo • Map P4 • Open 9am–1pm, 4–7pm Mon–Fri • Adm*

8 Museo Civico dell'Opera dei Pupi, Sortino
The collection is the patrimony of the Puglisi family, *pupari* for five generations. The master was Don Ignazio il Pastaro, who learned the family craft from his father and passed it down to his sons and grandsons. He built up the collection of puppets, scenery and manuscripts by purchasing entire workshops of famous *pupari* from the areas around Catania and Syracuse as they went out of business.
⊗ *Piazza S Francesco 9, Sortino • Map G5 • Opening times vary • Adm*

9 Assedio a Parigi
In this traditional story, Charlemagne, under siege by the Turks, sends Rinaldo to prepare the French army and Ruggero to Rome to ask assistance from the Pope. Ruggero spends the night at a castle where he is served a poisonous dinner and dies. Rinaldo defeats a group of Saracens and then the Turkish leader himself. The sorcerer Malagigi predicts Rinaldo's and Orlando's duel over Angelica and convinces the cousins to end their differences and head to Paris to fight the Saracens. Orlando saves the day.

10 The Defeat of Roncisvalle and the Death of Orlando
In another famous tale, Charlemagne is tricked by his brother-in-law Gano and sends the paladins, led by Orlando, to accompany his bishop who is to baptize a group of Saracens. But the paladins find themselves surrounded and outnumbered. After putting up a noble fight, Orlando dies on the battlefield.

Good Guys Orlando and Rinaldo

Left **Via della Libertà, Palermo** Right **Sciacca ceramics**

🔟 Specialist Shops and Areas

1 Palermo and Catania

On and around Palermo's Via della Libertà and Catania's Via Etnea you can shop in Italy's fashionable, classic stores for linens, clothing, shoes and handbags. Both boulevards offer a good mix of stores, boutiques and chic cafés.

2 Le Colonne, Taormina

Here you'll find elegant jewellery on Taormina's Corso. The proprietor makes each piece crafted to her own design, inspired by antique and historical motifs. Chunky necklaces of heavy gold with precious gems and rings set with antique incised stones are all unique items *(see p106)*.

The Corso, Taormina

3 Le Delizie di Elena, Castelvetrano

Rosemarie Ferlito and Tomas Schuster work with local organic farmers and oil millers to procure the highest quality Sicilian ingredients for their *sott'oli* – foods preserved under Nocellara del Belice olive oil. Artichokes and aubergines (eggplants) are cooked in vinegar and packed under a layer of olive oil. Sundried tomatoes are chopped fine and mixed with anchovies and *pecorino* cheese to make *cappuliato*. And it takes a total of four days to make *Corali di Sicilia* – small hot peppers stuffed with capers and anchovies. Their hand-made products are of the maximum quality and flavour.
◈ *Via Emilia • Map B3 • Open by appt only (tel: 0924 934 128)*

4 Enoteca Picone, Palermo

An excellent selection of Sicilian, Italian and international wines are for sale in this wonderful Palermo *enoteca*, and there's an area devoted to wine-tasting. Although wine is the focus, there are a few carefully selected food items as well, such as olive oil, pasta, honey and marmalade. If you want to relax and enjoy a glass or a bottle, visit their wine bar and restaurant near Piazza San Francesco d'Assisi *(see p87)*.

5 Sete d'Incanto, Syracuse

In her small studio, showroom and boutique on the island of Ortygia, designer Helene Moreau paints abstract watercolour designs onto silk. The resulting fabric is then made up into beautiful and highly unique scarves and dresses.
◈ *Via Roma 27 • Map H5*

Le Delizie di Elena sells its products via the Internet. Visit the website www.piaceriditalia.it

6 De Simone Ceramiche d'Arte, Palermo

Brightly coloured ceramics with designs of jolly peasant farmers and fishermen going about their daily tasks *(see p87)*.

7 Ceramiche d'Arte F.lli Soldano, Sciacca

Alongside shops selling Sciacca's traditional green, yellow and blue ceramic dishes, the Soldano family produces traditional ceramics and modern designs on tableware and tiles. ✆ *Piazza Saverio Friscia 17 • Map C4*

8 Silva Ceramica, Caltagirone

In a courtyard off the piazza Silva Ceramica produces imitations of antique designs, including tiles. ✆ *Piazza Umberto I, 19 • Map F4*

9 Altieri 1882, Erice

Altieri produces ceramics in traditional styles as well as their own innovative designs. There are also pieces in gold, silver and coral in the decorative arts tradition of Trapani *(see p96)*.

10 Pina Parisi Tappeti, Erice

Pina Parisi weaves cotton and wool rugs in traditional bright colours and geometric patterns as well as wall hangings of local village and countryside scenes *(see p96)*.

Pina Parisi Tappeti, Erice

Top 10 Markets

1 Trapani
Each morning fishermen arrange their silvery catch under the loggia, yelling out its merits or holding it aloft for the benefit of prospective clients. ✆ *Map B2*

2 Selinunte
A lively 7am fish auction. Not to be missed. ✆ *Map B4*

3 Ballerò, Palermo
Palermo's most interesting market sells fish, produce and household goods. ✆ *Map L6*

4 Del Capo, Palermo
Step back into 19th-century Palermo in the streets of the mandamento del Capo, crowded with farmers, housewives, butchers and every sort of meat imaginable. ✆ *Map J4*

5 Vucciria, Palermo
One of Palermo's oldest markets – vendors really put on a show. ✆ *Map M4*

6 Syracuse, Ortygia
Rows of mussels, cherries, almonds, lemons – or whatever is in season. ✆ *Map H5*

7 Sciacca
Fishermen arrive in the afternoon, Monday to Friday, to sell their catch on the wharf. ✆ *Map C4*

8 Donnalucata
Each morning, under brightly striped awnings along the wharf, fishermen sell their catch. ✆ *Map F6*

9 Catania
Catania's market is famous for the variety of fish and the rowdy vendors. ✆ *Map G4*

10 Impromptu Markets
All over Sicily, farmers sell their own produce from the side of the road. You're likely to find wild asparagus, lemons, artichokes and cheese.

Left **Bar Duomo, Cefalù** Right **Piazza A Scandaliato, Sciacca**

🔟 Nights Out

1 Discos
Discoteche open up each summer, often under new names and management. Huge crowds of visitors mix with locals who come from miles around to fill up the open-air dance floors and bars and the occasional billiard room. Look for posters for clubs in places such as Palermo, Marsala and Marzamemi.

2 The Piazza
In quiet villages, especially in summer when people stay inside during long, hot afternoons, families and friends get together in the piazza and eat *gelato* long into the night. In more touristy towns, the piazza assumes a pub atmosphere with live music and outdoor tables, such as The Bar Molo and Bar al Duomo at Cefalù.

Palermo nightlife

3 The Passeggiata
The *passeggiata* can be an afternoon or an evening activity. Join the crowds on the promenades at Selinunte, San Vito lo Capo, Mondello, Marina di Ragusa – or indeed anywhere a group might get together.

4 Summer Festivals
Cities and provinces organize great events to entertain tourists and locals all summer long. Ask at the local tourist offices or try to visit some of the following: Inykon at Menfi, with local foods, dancing, music and performances in the piazza in early June; Marsala Doc Jazz festival with wine and music in July; Estate Insieme with outdoor films and shows in Marsala in August; Sikula Reggae Festival at Rosolini in mid-August; and Palermo Summer Festival at the Fiera del Mediterraneo.

5 Kursaal Kalhesa, Palermo
Spend an evening in the cavernous spaces inside Palermo's old defensive walls. Kursaal Kalhesa serves dinner on an outdoor terrace, usually offers live jazz and has a wine bar and contemporary art inside *(see p88)*.

6 I Candelai, Palermo
This pub is popular with the 20-something crowd, sitting around tables on the pedestrianized street or in the large interior with space for live music and cabaret *(see p88)*.

For more on nightlife in Palermo **See p88**

7 Via Landolina, Catania

Via Landolina, near the Piazza Bellini, is lined with bars and clubs. Music is the focus at the bar La Chiave, which usually has a programme of live music and in summer organizes Landolina Live, a full slate of live rock, folk and jazz during June, July and August. ✎ *Map G4*

8 The Other Place Pub, Catania
University students crowd both storeys of this pub/pizzeria and the seats outside in summer. It's near the Piazza dell'Università, an area that has been over-hauled in the last few years thanks to the attentions of a progressive mayor. In the heart of the centre, from Piazza dell'Università to Piazza Bellini, there are literally hundreds of pubs and bars. ✎ *Via E Reina 18 • Map G4*

9 Vittorio Emanuele Birreria, Sciacca
In a nice piazza at the end of Sciacca's Corso sit out under palm trees enjoying the cool evening, live music, drinks and snacks. The setting is pure Sicily, with an up close and personal view of the Palazzo Steripinto across the street, with its deteriorating rustication and a single column articulating the corner. The Piazza A Scandaliato is also lively at night. ✎ *Corso at via Gerard • Map C4*

10 Lapis

This free publication lists complete offerings of music, theatre and art for Palermo and Catania. It's a good way to find information about summer festivals, and is available at tourist offices, cinemas, bars and cafés *(see p88)*.

Top 10 Features of the Passeggiata

1 The Walk

The key to the walk on the *passeggiata* is to do it *very* slowly.

2 See
Everybody checks out everybody else for everything from physical attributes, to fashion sense, to well-behaved children.

3 Be Seen
Wear the latest fashions including high, spiked heels for girls and high, spiked hair for guys.

4 When and Where
The prime time is Sunday afternoon or any day from dusk onwards. Walk around a piazza, down a corso or promenade, or anywhere people happen to gather.

5 Who
From babies in carriages to teens to grandparents, to entire families, couples and groups of friends, this is an open event.

6 The Touch
Everyone holds hands or entwines arms with their walking partners.

7 Food
The only things Italians consume while in motion are *gelato* or peanuts and the like.

8 Men with Earpieces
Pocket radios allow sports fans to stay abreast of the *partita* (football match) or Formula Uno motor racing.

9 By Car
Drive extremely slowly, with the windows rolled down so that you can chat.

10 Spectator Sport
Feel free to sit and watch the *passeggiata* go by, but sit side by side facing the action.

Left **Bread** Right **Gambero rosso**

TOP 10 Sicilian Dishes

1 Bread

Bread is a ritual in Sicily. Made from *grano duro* (semolina flour), once baked it is dense and golden, unlike any other bread in Italy. The shapes are particular to Sicily too, including braided loaves, and topped with sesame seeds. Bread is also used in main dishes – *mollica*, which are spiced and toasted breadcrumbs, often substitute for cheese on top of pasta. Also look for *sfincione*, similar to a thick crust pizza eaten as a snack, and *focaccie*, thin baked layers of dough filled with greens, sausage, ricotta or tomato.

2 Pasta

The amazing variety of pasta dishes makes use of all the bounty Sicily has to offer. A typical Palermitan dish is *pasta con le sarde* (with sardines, fennel, pine nuts, raisins and anchovies). The pasta itself, made with local durum wheat, is firm and full of flavour.

Pasta con le sarde

3 Risotto

Rice dishes are as plentiful as pasta, and are particularly good with Sicilian lemons, *nero di sepia* (cuttlefish ink), greens or prawns. A real treat is the elaborate *Rippiddu Annivicatu*: rice is blackened with squid ink and shaped in a mound to resemble Mount Etna, a topping of ricotta cheese evokes the snowcap, and tomatoes the flames and lava flows.

4 Fish and Seafood

There is always an excellent choice of fish and seafood in Sicily. Look out for *soglia* (flounder), *triglie* (red mullet), *pesce spada* (swordfish), *tonno* (tuna), *mazzancolla* (large sweet prawns), *aragosta* (spiny lobster), *sarde* (sardines), *polpo* (octopus), *calamaro* (squid) and *gambero rosso* (red prawns).

5 Meat

Excellent lamb and pork are produced in Sicily. Sausages are always spiced and made with *finocchio* (fennel seeds), stuffed in narrow casings and formed into continuous coils.

6 Caponata

Originally a fish dish, it was adapted by the *cucina povera* (kitchen of the poor) as a slow-cooked mix of aubergine (eggplant), tomato, celery, capers, olives, raisins and pine nuts, flavoured with vinegar and sugar, and topped with toasted almonds.

7 Arancini
A Sicilian fast-food treat, available in bars and from street vendors. Balls of rice are stuffed with a meaty tomato ragout, rolled in breadcrumbs, and fried. Their round, golden shapes resemble oranges (aranci), hence their name.

8 Panelle
Another snack food available from street vendors are these small squares of fried batter made from chickpea flour and a sprinkling of parsley, then topped with salt and lemon juice.

9 Gelato
What makes Sicilian ice cream (gelato) so special is its base: a crema developed from Arab and Spanish culinary influences made with milk, or almond milk, and starch. It produces a rich, smooth and light dessert (see p100).

10 Cassata and Cannoli
These classic Sicilian desserts are both made with lightly sweetened ricotta. The cassata combines creamy ricotta and sponge cake covered with green and white marzipan and decorated with candied fruits. Cannoli are lightly fried pastry shells filled with ricotta.

Local Produce

1 Cheese
Sicilian cheese comes from cows' or sheep's (pecorino) milk. Look for primo sale, aged pecorino, tuma, caciocavallo and Ragusana.

2 Ricotta
A cheese by-product used for sweet and savoury dishes. Available fresh, baked, or salted and aged (ricotta salata).

3 Capers
From tiny capers to the huge cucunci, the best come from Salina and Pantelleria.

4 Vegetables
Amazing bounty awaits at marketplaces and restaurants. Don't miss the long skinny cucuzza (squash) and spicy red garlic.

5 Citrus Fruits
Excellent lemons (there is a small, sweet variety) and oranges (with numerous blood-red varieties) abound.

6 Salt
Richly flavoured salt has been harvested from the sea near Trapani since Phoenician times (see p04).

7 Durum Wheat
The secret behind Sicily's flavourful bread and pasta. The countryside is covered with wheat fields.

8 Almonds and Pistachios
Eastern Sicily is known for its production of these high-quality and richly flavoured nuts.

9 Tuna
You'll find this fish in every form: fresh, preserved in oil, and in a variety of cuts.

10 Olives and Olive Oil
Millions of olive trees produce excellent quality table olives and thick, green aromatic olive oil.

Cannoli

Left **Barrels of Marsala wine** Right **Alcamo vineyards**

🔟 Wines and Wine Producers

1 Nero d'Avola
The classic Sicilian red, made from at least 80 per cent of grapes of the same name with added Perricone, is characterized by its intense ruby colour and flavour of aromatic herbs. It's produced over the entire eastern half of the island but the two largest producers are between Palermo and Cefalù: Regaleali and Duca di Salaparuta.

2 Bianco d'Alcamo
Eighty per cent Catarratto with a dash of Damaschino, Grecanico and Trebbiano make up this dry and fruity white. Abundant production (more grapes are grown in Trapani than any other Sicilian province) made this the classic Sicilian white. The area from San Vito Lo Capo to Castellammare and inland to Alcamo and Calatafimi is under DOC *(Denominazione di Origine Controllata)* protection.

3 Marsala
A fortified wine produced in Marsala since the 18th century *(see p92)*. Awarded a DOC in 1986, Marsala is produced as Fine, Superiore (aged at least two years), Riserva (aged at least four years) or Vergine and Soleras (aged at least 10 years). Made from Grillo, Catarratto and Inzolia grapes, the wine is amber with a rich perfume of citrus flowers and almonds.

Cerasuolo wine label

4 Cerasuolo di Vittoria
The cherry-red, dry and fruity wine is made from a blend of Frappato, Calabrese and Nerello grapes grown near Vittoria in the province of Ragusa. Established producers are buying vineyards in the area to produce their own versions of Cerasuolo.

5 Malvasia and Passito
Producers on Salina leave their Malvasia delle Lipari grapes to dry out on the vine or on mats to concentrate the flavours to make a sweet, thick dessert wine. Pantelleria's Zibbibo grapes are treated in a similar way, left on the vine until the flavours have condensed to make a dessert wine with intense tastes of dried fruits and vanilla.

Marsala

6 Etna Bianco and Etna Rosso

Sicily's first DOC was awarded in 1968 to the southern and eastern zone of Mount Etna where the white grapes Cataratto and Carricante flourish. Reds, mostly the Nerello Mascalese, grow around the volcano's base.

7 Regealali

The estate near Vallelunga has been in the Tasca d'Almerita family since 1830. Alongside traditional Sicilian wines Regealali also bottles international varieties. Their reds, based on Nero d'Avola, include Regealali Rosso and the Rosso del Conte; whites primarily of Inzolia and their own Varietà Tasca, include Villa Tasca and Nozze d'Oro.

Regealali white wine

8 Marco de Bartoli

Marco de Bartoli and his sons cultivate indigenous grapes and remain faithful to the traditions of their area. Their production includes classic Marsalas and the unfortified Vecchio Samperi, aged for 20 or 30 years.

9 Planeta

At his estate near Sambuca di Sicilia, Diego Planeta and family plant both indigenous and international grapes – taste La Segreta Rosso (Nero d'Avola with Merlot and Syrah).

10 Small Producers

Many small producers are making excellent wines. Look out for Fondo Antico, Cusumano, Racalmare di Morgante, Rudinì and Calabretta, among others.

Top 10 Grape Varieties

1 Nero d'Avola
The powerhouse Sicilian red grape, cultivated in the eastern half of the island.

2 Frappato
Cultivated in the province of Ragusa, the primary grape of Cerasuolo di Vittoria.

3 Grillo
A white grape indigenous to western Sicily and the basis of Marsala and other whites.

4 Inzolia
Also called Ansonica, a white grape throughout western Sicily, used in Marsala and other wines.

5 Zibbibo
The grape of Pantelleria, used for white wines and predominantly for the rich, full bodied *passito*.

6 Nerrello Mascalese
Primary red grape grown on the slopes of Mount Etna, blended with Nerello Cappuccio to make the deep, spicy Etna Rosso.

7 Malvasia di Lipari
Responsible for the fragrant wines of Salina, rich in flavours of almond and candied fruits.

8 Catarratto
A white grape all over the island, changing character depending on the micro-climate. Grown from Marsala to Alcamo, Salina and Etna.

9 Grecanico
White grape native to western Sicily and one of the primary components of Bianco d'Alcamo.

10 International Vines
Recent additions to Sicilian vineyards include Chardonnay, Cabernet Sauvignon, Merlot and Syrah.

 Visits can be arranged to Regealali estate (tel. 091 64 59 7110, Planeta (tel. 091 32 965) and Marco de Bartoli (tel. 0923 96 20 93).

Left **Pasticceria Gelateria F Colicchia, Trapani** Right **Caffè Sicilia, Noto**

Pasticcerie and Gelaterie

1 Caffè Sicilia, Noto
For more than a century the family of Carlo and Corrado Assenza have been behind the marble counter and at work in the maze-like laboratory of the Caffè Sicilia. The brothers are purists and hunt down the highest quality ingredients Sicily has to offer, working to preserve the Sicilian pastry-making tradition. They create pastries from the recipes of Noto's ex-monastery of Santa Chiara as well as from their own innovative recipes, such as chocolates with carob, chestnut or sweet basil filling, *giuggiolena* (sesame seed, honey and orange zest bar) and herb-infused honey. ◈ *Corso Vittorio Emanuele 125 • Map G5*

2 Pasticceria Gelateria F Colicchia, Trapani
The oldest pastry shop in Trapani, run by three generations of the Colicchia family. Their summertime speciality is *granita* served with an aniseed biscuit; in winter you'll find the best *cannoli* in Sicily. ◈ *Via delle Arti 6–8 & via Carosio 30–32 • Map B2*

3 Cistercian Monastery, Agrigento
The nuns at the monastery of the Santo Spirito still offer pastries from behind the grate. They may look like something you've seen at other shops, but take a bite and taste how special they are. Order ahead for the speciality, "cous cous" *(see p26)*.

4 Pasticceria Artigianale Grammatico Maria, Erice
Maria Grammatico spent many years in the orphanage inside Erice's cloistered San Carlo monastery, learning the nuns' centuries-old recipes for their *dolci*, the sale of which provided their keep. The sweets are the opposite of monastic life: colourful and luxurious – try *sospiri* (sighs), *cuore* (hearts) and *cuscinetti* (little pillows). ◈ *Via Vittorio Emanuele 14 • Map B2*

5 Donna Elvira Dolceria, Modica
Elvira Roccasalva has a passion for traditional recipes, faithfully reproducing by hand the sweets formerly made by Modica's cloistered nuns. She also uses the best-quality ingredients from the region to create her own recipes: try the *carato*, made with carob flour, raisins and almonds. ◈ *Corso Umberto I, 156 • Map G6*

Typical Sicilian granite ices

6 Antica Dolceria Bonajuto, Modica

Fig-filled *nucatoli* and citrus and honey *torrone* are displayed in a small, elegant shop located off Modica's Corso. Their chocolate is still made using the ancient Aztec method of working the cocoa mass with sugar and spices. ✎ *Corso Umberto I, 159 • Map G6*

7 Gelateria Stancampiano, Palermo

This unassuming family-owned shop has the most excessively creamy *gelato* in Sicily. The bow-tied staff proudly offer rows and rows of traditional and seasonal flavours served up in cones, cups and brioches. In summer it is open 24 hours a day. ✎ *Via E Notarbarolo 51 • Map K2*

8 Antico Caffè di Spinnato, Palermo

A classic pastry shop and bar offering a wide range of sweets, biscuits, breads, *gelato* and *arancini (see p71)*. Sit in the elegant tearoom or on the pedestrianized street. ✎ *Via Principe di Belmonte 115 • Map K2*

9 Pasticceria Russo, Catania

Since 1880 the Russo family has been producing Catanese pastries using the finest of local ingredients, including pistachios, almonds, oranges and honey. ✎ *Via Vittorio Emanuele 105, Santa Venerina • Map G4*

10 Pasticceria Svizzera Caviezel, Catania

The Caviezel family came to Catania from Switzerland in 1914 to make Swiss pastries. Now their recipes have been Sicilianized, although French buttercream still features in their pastries. ✎ *Corso Italia 123 • Map G4*

Top 10 Desserts

1 Cassata
Layers of sponge cake and ricotta cream covered with colourful marzipan and candied fruits *(see p71)*.

2 Gelato
Try soft and creamy ice cream, *zabaglione, semifreddo,* or the solid *pezzo duro*.

3 Granita
Gelato's older cousin, ice is added to flavourings such as jasmine, wild strawberry or almond.

4 Biancomangiare
A snow-white pudding from Arab and Spanish days made with almond milk or cow's milk and thickened with rice starch.

5 Cannolo
Ricotta cream in a fried pastry tube *(see p71)*.

6 Frutta di Martorana
Almond paste sculpted and painted to look like real fruit or other edibles.

7 Biscotti della Regina
Hard biscuits rolled in sesame seeds.

8 Cassateddi
Fried pockets filled with ricotta flavoured with chocolate, lemon or cinnamon, eaten at breakfast time.

9 Coseduce or Cuccidati
Traditional fig-filled biscuits that exist under various names in every part of the island. Elaborate versions are made for St Joseph's Day *(see p56)* and called *squartucciati*.

10 'mpanatigghi
These Modican pastries imported by the Spanish Counts of Modica are *empanadas,* a pastry crust filled with chocolate, spices and ground beef.

Left **Santandrea** Right **Ristorante Gangivecchio**

ꜱ:10 Restaurants

1 Ristorante Duomo, Ragusa

Chef Ciccio Sultano carefully selects each ingredient with which to prepare dishes faithful to Ragusan tradition, but with his own twist. In three small, bright, elegant dining rooms, every course is excellent, starting with the bread basket. Two different tasting menus let you try a bit of everything *(see p125)*.

2 Santandrea, Palermo

In a narrow lane a few steps from Palermo's Piazza San Domenico, Santandrea is set in a renovated building where the exposed terracotta, antique rugs, wooden floors and tables create a warm atmosphere. In fine weather tables are set in the piazzetta under the crumbling façade of the church of Sant'Andrea. The friendly staff explain the menu and the Palermitan food is excellent, including interesting pastas, simple and well prepared fresh fish and good desserts *(see p89)*.

Typical Sicilian fish dish

3 Locanda del Borgo, Rosolini

The Locanda has accurately restored a few rooms of the local prince's castle in this tiny village. They also authentically follow traditional methods in the kitchen. Dishes are innovative mixes of inland vegetables with fish from the nearby sea, each prepared to achieve a harmony of freshness, flavour and texture. Try the *cuccia* (cracked wheat, white cabbage and sea snails) or pistachio ravioli with crustaceans and cacao beans *(see p125)*.

4 Ristorante Fidone Maria, Friginitini

Maria Fidone and family are in the kitchen at their homely *trattoria*, preparing hearty Ragusan dinners. Everything is made in-house including the pasta, bread, olive oil, wines and liqueurs. For a first course choose the thick fava bean soup *(lolli)* or home-made pasta. For a second course try stuffed chicken accompanied by stuffed aubergines (egg-plants)*(see p125)*.

5 Ristorante Gangivecchio, Gangi

In a restored monastery in the Madonie mountains, cookbook authors Wanda and Giovanna Tornabene prepare excellent mountain fare. Pasta with a fava purée, local rabbit and lamb and desserts such as *arancini* filled with ricotta are all paired with local wines *(see p107)*.

6 Il Cuciniera, Catania

Modican chef Carmelo Chiaramonte is devoted to the Sicilian foods from the peasant farmer traditions of Ragusa, Syracuse and Catania, and particularly to the produce from Mount Etna. With authentic local ingredients as a base, he creates new dishes of meat, fish, wild fruits and green vegetables. The wine list includes more than 20 labels from Etna *(see p107)*.

7 Il Dehor de l'Hotel Foresteria Baglio della Luna, Agrigento

Owner Ignazio Altieri makes his clients feel at home, whether on the terrace with views of the Valle dei Templi or in the cool, wood-panelled and brocade dining room. The cuisine is modern Italian with an international twist although the menu makes the dishes seem more complicated than they are. Try prawn risotto or grilled tuna with cous cous *(see p115)*.

8 Ristorante Bar La Pineta, Selinunte

This daytime bar transforms itself into a romantic restaurant by night. Tables are set out on the sandy beach, lit by torches, and fish caught by Selinunte's fishermen make up the menu. Try steamed clams and mussels or lobster fettuccini *(see p97)*.

9 Pocho, San Vito lo Capo

You can't do better for a view than the terrace at Pocho, with Monte Cofano and the bay splayed out before you. Owner Marilù Terrasi is well-known for her cous cous and the wine list is made up of selected Sicilian labels *(see p97)*.

10 Ai Lumi Tavernetta, Trapani

The cozy dining room in this "little tavern" is decorated with old farm implements. The menu is full of local specialities such as pasta in a garlic and tomato sauce with basil and almonds *(see p97)*.

Ai Lumi Tavernetta sign

AROUND SICILY

SICILY'S TOP 10

Left **Museo Archeologico** Right **Palermo market stall**

Palermo

SETTLED BY THE PHOENICIANS IN THE 8TH CENTURY BC, *Palermo fell first to the Romans, then the Arabs, who chose Palermo for their capital, making the city one of the most magnificent and powerful in the world. This splendour was compounded during the Norman reign. Today what remains of earlier ages coexists with modern life: laundry billows off balconies of 15th-century palaces; buses rumble past even older buildings displaying a mix of east and west. Buildings destroyed in World War II have been left open to the sky, but Sicilians are ever resourceful: restaurants seat diners in crumbling, yet romantic courtyards while a bombed-out church is used as an arts venue.*

🔟 Sights

1. Norman Palermo
2. Quattro Canti
3. La Martorana & San Cataldo
4. San Domenico
5. Museo Archeologico
6. La Kalsa
7. Palazzo Abatellis
8. La Cala & Piazza Marina
9. Albergheria
10. The New City

La Martorana and San Cataldo

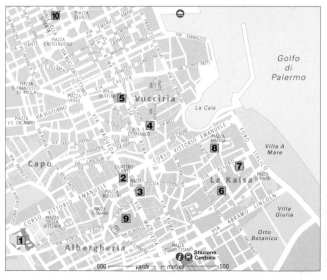

1 Norman Palermo

The splendid Norman kingdom in Sicily was marked by an exotic mix of cultures as manifested in their administration and in the architecture of the civic and private structures they commissioned (see pp8–9).

2 Quattro Canti

The heart of town is marked by the intersection of the via Maqueda and the via Vittorio Emanuele. Called the Quattro Canti (the four corners that divide Palermo into quadrants) each is swathed in sculptural decoration. The town hall is in the Piazza Pretoria just steps from the Quattro Canti, although the square is more commonly referred to as the Piazza Vergogna (Square of Shame), after the shameless nudes perched around the edge of the elaborate fountain. Currently under restoration, the fountain was sculpted by Tuscan Francesco Camilliani around 1555 and was originally intended for a Florentine garden, but was then moved down south. ◈ Map L6

3 La Martorana and San Cataldo

In Piazza Bellini are two splendid churches. The little, mid-12th-century San Cataldo has three Arabic bulbous red domes all in a row, latticed windows and an elegantly bare interior. But it is the Santa Maria dell' Ammiraglio next door that is the real gem. It was later renamed La Martorana after the Spanish patron who established a convent nearby. Notice the Norman bell tower (c.1140), now missing its red dome, which is just as dramatic as the Baroque façade added in the 16th century. Inside, ignore the later paintings in favour of

the original mosaic decoration by skilled Byzantine craftsmen. Just inside the door, an image of King Roger, feet firmly on the ground, is shown being personally crowned by Christ, hovering in his ethereal realm (see p44). ◈ Piazza Bellini 3 • Map M5 • Open 9:30am–1pm, 3:30–5:30pm daily • Free

4 San Domenico Church and Oratory of San Domenico and the Vucciria

A warren of little streets lies northeast of the Quattro Canti, home to the Vucciria market (see p67). Bordering the market to the north is the Church of San Domenico, burial place of notable Sicilians (see p44). Rebuilt in the Baroque style in 1640, the harmonious yellow-and-white façade is 18th century. Behind the church is the Baroque chapel, the Oratorio del Rosario di San Domenico, with an altarpiece by Anthony Van Dyck. ◈ Church of San Domenico: Piazza S Domenico; Map M3; Open 9–11:30am daily; Free • Oratorio del Rosario di San Domenico: Via dei Bambinai, Map M3; Open 9am–11:30am daily (ask the custodian at No. 16); Free

Oratorio del Rosario di San Domenico

Museo Archeologico

5 Palermo's regional archaeology museum displays finds from archaeological sites all over western Sicily, from the Neolithic age through to the Roman period. Among Punic and Egyptian objects is the Palermo Stone (c.2700 BC) with a hieroglyphic inscription recording a delivery of 40 boat-loads of Sicilian lumber to an Egyptian Pharaoh. There are also numerous Etruscan artifacts, Greek vases and Greek and Roman sculpture, but the highlight of the collection are the Archaic and Classical *metopes* recovered from Selinunte *(see pp30–33)*. ◈ *Piazza Olivella • Map L3 • Open 9am–2pm Mon, Wed, Thu, Sat; 9am–1pm, 3–6pm Tue & Fri; 9am–1pm Sun • Adm*

La Kalsa

6 The Arabs established their government in this area and its narrow, winding streets later became a densely populated residential district. Sadly, it was heavily bombed during World War II and few of the buildings have been restored, yet their crumbling state seems to add to the atmosphere in this bustling part of the city. Highlights include the Baroque Santa Teresa, the Santa Maria dello Spasimo dating from 1506, the restored 1151 Norman church of La Magione, later headquarters of the Teutonic knights, and the Catalan-Gothic Palazzo Aiutamicristo. Sicilians are ever resourceful and today many of the ruined buildings are being used inventively as restaurants and galleries. Stay alert if you're wandering this area at night. ◈ *Bordered by Foro Italico, via Lincoln, Garibaldi & Alloro • Map N5*

Palazzo Abatellis

7 Sicily's regional fine arts museum is housed in the heavily restored 15th-century palace of a Spanish official, deep in the La Kalsa neighbourhood. The permanent collection traces the development of the figurative tradition in Sicilian art and the museum runs an active exhibition programme. Highlights include the door and courtyard of the building itself, a masterpiece of Gothic-Catalan architecture, the detached fresco of the *Triumph of Death* by an unknown 15th-century master, carved works by Antonello Gagini, Antonello da Messina's *Annunciation to the Virgin*, and an enormous 14th-century Hispano-Moresque amphora *(see p38)*. ◈ *Via Alloro 4 • Map P4 • Open 9am–1:30pm Mon & Wed, 9am–1:30pm, 3–7:30pm Tue, Thu, Fri & Sat; 9am–12:30pm Sun • Adm*

Triumph of Death fresco, Palazzo Abatellis

Yachts, Palermo port

8 La Cala & Piazza Marina
Yachts bobbing in the small port can be seen from the 15th-century church of Santa Maria della Catena, while palaces of Palermo's aristocracy line the Piazza Marina. In the centre of the lovely gardens is a statue of Garibaldi *(see p37)*. The 1582 Porta Felice leads out to the Foro Italico and the seafront, for good waterside walks. ✿ *Map N3*

9 Albergheria
Bordered by via Vittorio Emanuele and via Maqueda, this rather poor residential area is a maze of streets spanned with billowing laundry. The heart of the neighbourhood is given over to the Ballarò market *(see p67)*. Don't miss the 17th century Chiesa del Carmine on via Giovanni Grasso with its stuccoed interior and frilly, polychrome cupola. ✿ *Map L6*

10 The New City
The wide, tree-lined boulevard via della Libertà travels west from the Teatro Politeama, where the sparkling modern city begins, full of shops and cafés. It passes the Giardino Inglese, laid out with palms, to Piazza Vittorio Veneto and the entrance to the public gardens. ✿ *Map J1*

A Morning in La Kalsa and Albergheria

🕙 From via Maqueda take the Piazza Santa Quaranta Martiri up to the Chiesa del Gesù for a look at the wild Baroque decoration of the interior. Beyond the church, enter the streets taken over by **Ballarò market** *(see p67)* and spend some time weaving your way through the overloaded stalls. For a late breakfast stop at one of the stalls serving *arancini (see p71)* or fried aubergine (eggplant) sandwiches.

From Piazza Ballarò, pass through the old neighbourhood and by the Church of the Carmine with its colourful dome and take the via Case Nuove to via Maqueda. Head into **La Kalsa** on via Gorizia to via Garibaldi 43, where you can still see parts of the magnificent original structure of the Palazzo Aiutamicristo. Continue down to Santa Maria dello Spasimo where there may be contemporary art on view. Take the residential via della Vetreria to via Alloro, and tour the regional fine arts museum in **Palazzo Abatellis**.

Exit the museum and go south on via Alloro until the Piazza d'Aragona and take a right into via A. Paternostro to the Piazza San Francesco. Have lunch at the **Antica Focacceria** *(see p89)*, sitting in the piazza under the Gothic façade of San Francesco, or in the marble and wrought-iron interior, where you can watch the chefs serving up Sicilian specialities. For dessert, there's always good *gelato* to be found in the shop in the piazza.

Following pages **Baroque villa, Bagheria** (see p94)

Left **Museo Marionette** Right **Mondello**

Best of the Rest

1 Porta Nuova
This gateway to the city was erected in 1535 as a triumphal arch to commemorate Charles V's victory in Tunis. ◈ *Map J6*

2 Oratorio di Santa Zita
The interior of this chapel is covered with stucco decoration and Giacomo Serpotta's masterpiece of Biblical and historical scenes (c.1600). ◈ *Via Valverde 3 • Map M3 • Open 9am–1pm, 2–7pm Mon–Fri; 9am–1pm Sat • Free*

3 Palazzo Mirto
One of the few surviving aristocratic *palazzi* in Palermo. The lavish interior is intact with furnishings from the 18th and 19th centuries. ◈ *Via Merlo 2 • Map N4 • Open 9am–1pm, 3–6:30pm Mon–Sat, 9am–12:30pm Sun • Adm*

4 Castello della Zisa
From the Arabic *al-Aziz* (splendid), the palace lives up to its name. Arab craftsmen incorporated stalactite ceilings, interior fountains, mosaic decoration and an ingenious ventilation system. ◈ *Piazza Guglielmo il Buono • Open 9am–1pm, 3–7pm Mon–Sat; 9am–noon Sun • Adm*

5 Mandamento del Capo
This old neighbourhood winds around behind the cathedral down to via Maqueda. A residential area with bars, a puppet theatre and a good food market, it's a slice of Palermo's inner-city life. ◈ *Map K4*

6 Galleria d'Arte Moderna
A collection of contemporary works by Sicilian masters. ◈ *Teatro Politeama, via Turati • Map K1 • Open 9am–1pm Tue–Sun • Adm*

7 Museo Marionette
An extensive collection of worldwide puppet traditions (see p64). ◈ *Via Butera 1 • Map N4 • Open 9am–1pm, 4–7pm Mon–Sat • Adm*

8 Museo Pitrè
Founded in 1909 by Giuseppe Pitrè, chronicler of Sicilian customs, the museum preserves objects such as folk art and furniture. ◈ *Via Duca di Abruzzi • Open 9am–1pm Mon–Thu, Sat–Sun • Adm*

9 Cappuccini Catacombs
Burial ground of Palermo's upper classes (1599–1881); the niches still contain skeletons. ◈ *Via Cappuccini • Open 9am–noon, 3–5pm daily • Adm*

10 Mondello
This fishing village became a fashionable resort in the 19th century (see p50). ◈ *Map D2*

Left **Via della Libertà** Right **De Simone ceramics**

Places to Shop

Via della Libertà
Up-scale Italian chains line the boulevard between the Teatro Politeama and Piazza Crispi: try Frette for linens, Furla for leather goods, Pollini for shoes, Richard Ginori for housewares, and Max Mara for women's fashions. ◈ *Map J1*

Via Enrico Parisi
Just off via della Libertà find chic boutiques such as Visiona, (Nos. 11–13) with ultra modern fashion, and Geneviève Lethu, (No. 7a) with French housewares. Stop in at the equally chic Il Baretto (No. 43) for an *aperitivo* or a bite to eat. ◈ *Map J1*

De Simone
The de Simone family has been producing high-quality hand-painted ceramics for generations, with designs illustrating jolly Sicilian farmers and fishermen. ◈ *Via Daita' 13 • Map K1*

Vincenzo Argento
For four generations the Argento family has been practising the art of puppetry. They make traditional puppets in the Palermitan style for sale and for use in their nearby theatre. ◈ *Corso Vittorio Emanuele 445 • Map L5*

Rinascente and Coin
Outlets of Italy's two main department stores are located across the street from one another. Rinascente has a more up-market image, but both have good selections of Italian clothing and particularly good houseware departments. ◈ *Via Ruggiero Settimo • Map K2*

Enoteca Picone
Wine has been the Picone family business since 1946. In their large *enoteca* they offer a selection of Sicilian wines plus international labels for sale, facilities for tasting and a few selected food items *(see p89)*. ◈ *Via G Marconi 36 • Map J1*

Mangia Delicatessen
Plenty of speciality items in a small space: cold cuts and cheese; wine; olive oil; marmalade; tuna and more. ◈ *Via Principe di Belmonte 116 • Map L2*

Spirale Shop
The studio of Roberto Intorro, Iano Chiavetta and Toni Bonura, three artists working in metal. Playful jewellery, candle holders and wall hangings. ◈ *Via Bara all'Olivella 115 • Map L3*

Via Bara all'Olivella
Visit the showrooms of Cobbola, where the beret is given new life, Ippobosco for miniatures of Sicilian homes, plus other shops with funky lamps and ceramics. ◈ *Map L3*

Markets
Some of the best shopping in Palermo happens at the three daily food markets and the antique/flea market *(see p67)*.

For tips on shopping in Sicily **See p133**

Left **Teatro Massimo** Right **Outdoor bar, Piazza Olivella**

Nights Out

1 Teatro Massimo
Palermo's historic theatre opened in 1897 then went into decline, but it was reopened in 1997 after a major restoration effort. It stages lyrical opera, ballet and symphonic concerts.
⊗ *Piazza Verdi • Map K3 • Guided tours*

2 Teatro di Verdura
A summer season of opera, ballet, concerts and plays is presented in this outdoor theatre in the garden of the former villa of the Prince of Castelnuovo.
⊗ *Viale del Fante 70b • Map N1*

3 Teatro Politeama Garibaldi
The theatre was designed in 1874 in Neo-Classical style. The season offers symphonic concerts and ballet. ⊗ *Piazza Ruggero Settimo • Map K2 • Concerts 5:15pm & 9:15pm*

4 Teatro Biondo Stabile
Founded by the Biondo brothers in 1903 as a centre for experimental theatre, it is still fulfilling its mission. ⊗ *Via Teatro Biondo 11 • Map M4*

5 Santa Maria dello Spasimo
Lo Spasimo is a bombed-out church that acts as an amazing venue for an art gallery and a full programme of films and concerts (classical, contemporary, jazz), romantically staged in the roofless nave and garden space out the back. ⊗ *Via Spasimo, Piazza Magione • Map P5 • Open 9am–midnight daily • Free*

6 Kursaal Kalhesa
Located inside of Palermo's defensive walls in an enormous, arched space is this bar, restaurant, bookshop and jazz venue all combined. There are cubbyholes for hiding out, a fireplace in winter and a terrace in summer.
⊗ *Foro Umberto I, 21 • Map P2*

7 I Candelai
This pub is tucked in along a pedestrian street where candlemakers' shops used to be. There are tables outside in the street and live music or floor shows performed in the spacious interior. ⊗ *Via dei Candelai 65 • Map L4*

8 Malox
Not far from I Candelai, tables are set outside in the little piazza. Music is the focus here, with jazz jamming sessions and up-and-coming Italian rock groups.
⊗ *Piazzetta della Canna 8–9 • Map L4*

9 Piazza Olivella
At night the piazza between Teatro Massimo and via Cavour fills up with university students hanging out in the many bars lining the square. ⊗ *Map L3*

10 Lapis
Check this free publication for listings of all music, theatre and art happenings in Palermo, including summer music festivals organized in the Giardini Inglese and Fiera del Mediterraneo. Available at tourist offices, cinemas, bars and cafés.

Above **Santandrea**

Price Categories

For a three-course	€	under €25
meal for one with half	€€	€25–€35
a bottle of wine (or	€€€	€35–€55
equivalent meal), taxes	€€€€	€55–€70
and extra charges.	€€€€€	over €70

🔟 Places to Eat

1 Santandrea
In the Vucciria market, Santandrea offers dishes with a twist, such as pasta with squid, fava beans and orange peel (see p76). ◎ Piazzetta Sant' Andrea 4 • Map M4 • 091-334 999 • Closed Tue • €€€

2 Trattoria Stella
Making the most of the situation, Stella is set in a former hotel in the bombed-out La Kalsa neighbourhood. Spend the evening in the crumbling yet romantic courtyard under palms and jasmine. ◎ Via Alloro 104 • Map P4 • 091-616 11 36 • Closed Tue • €€

3 Il Macco
Just behind the Politeama is this unassuming trattoria. The signature dish is il macco, a purée of fava beans with fennel and tomato ◎ Via R Gravina 85 • Map L1 • 340-526 35 87 • No credit cards • Closed Sun • €

4 Mi Manda Picone
In an inviting, arched interior, the trattoria of the Enoteca Picone (see p87) serves snacks and full meals, accompanied by their excellent wines. ◎ Via A Paternostro 69 • Map M4 • 091-616 06 60 • Closed Sun • €€

5 Antica Focacceria
Palermitan fast food under the façade of San Francesco. Sandwiches, panelle (see p71), focaccia and pasta. ◎ Via A Paternostro 58 (Piazza S Francesco) • Map M4 • 091-320 264 • No credit cards • €

6 Al Genio
Another Palermitan favourite, with tables set in a courtyard. Try pasta with swordfish, mint and almonds. ◎ Piazza S Carlo 9 • Map N5 • 091-616 66 42 • Closed Sun • €

7 Kursaal Kalhesa
Fresh food using prime ingredients of Sicily (see p88). ◎ Foro Umberto I, 21 • Map P2 • 091-616 22 82 • Closed Sun D, Mon L • €€€

8 Capricci di Sicilia
Everything is good here – try aubergines (eggplants) stuffed with mint and garlic. ◎ Piazza Sturzo 6 • Map K1 • 091-327 777 • €€

9 Gusto DiVino
Creatively prepared fish and seafood flavoured with, for example, honey and pistachio. ◎ Corso Pisani 30 • Map L6 • 091-645 70 01 • Closed Sun • €€€

10 Bye Bye Blues
Excellent Sicilian ingredients are chosen for inventive dishes. ◎ Via del Garofolo 23, Mondello • Map D2 • 091-684 14 15 • Closed Tue • €€€

> **Note:** Unless otherwise stated, all restaurants accept credit cards and serve vegetarian meals

Left **Selinunte** Right **Trapani harbour**

Northwest Sicily

FAR FROM THE DEVELOPED RESORTS OF THE EAST COAST, *much of this area was remote until relatively recently and presents unique opportunities to wander through fishing villages, watch shepherds at work and witness a way life that has survived for centuries. The coastal areas and offshore islands are pristine, while the mountainous interior, part rocky, part arable, has some of the harshest terrain in Sicily – water is scarce, the heat relentless and earthquakes are not infrequent. The villages of the interior lost large percentages of their population to mass emigration over the last century (see p37) but those who remain are largely small farmers still using mules to work their fields, or younger generations turning their talents towards developing vineyards of local grapes to produce high-quality Sicilian wines.*

🔟 Sights

1. Monreale
2. Selinunte
3. Trapani
4. Segesta
5. Lo Zingaro
6. Pantelleria
7. Marsala
8. Motya
9. Egadi Islands
10. Erice

Marsala

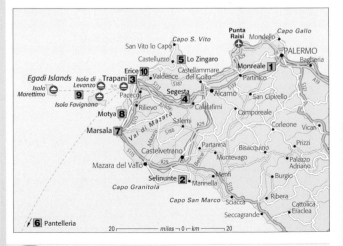

Cloister, Monreale

Monreale
1 On this royal hill *(mons reale)* Sicily's Norman king, William II, built the mosaic-encrusted monastery and cathedral that proved to be the last and most splendid of the island's Norman monuments *(see pp10–11)*.

Selinunte
2 The ruins of this Greek city, including temples, walls, market-place and homes, stand majesti-cally backed by the sea – silent reminders of the glory of the once great city *(see pp30–33)*.

Trapani
3 A busy port since the Phoenicians landed here, it gained importance during Spanish domination as the closest port to Spain, and it's still a bustling area. The modern town has ballooned, but the quaint and lively historic centre is concentrated on the tiny sickle-shaped peninsula – the entire area covers less than 2.5 sq km (1 sq mile). The perpendicular main streets are lined with a mix of Baroque buildings, shops and cafés. Via Torrearsa leads from the port to the market square with its lovely loggia. The Corso leads to the tip of the peninsula, with glimpses of everyday Sicilian life in the side streets. ® *Map B2*

Segesta
4 The most romantic ruins in all of Sicily are tucked between the green hills and rugged moun-tains just west of Calatafimi. The temple was built in perfect, solid Doric proportions (c.420 BC) and stands isolated on a gentle slope, turning a beautiful shade of pink in the sunset. The un-grooved columns, missing *cella*, and still-attached studs around the *stylobate* hint that it was left unfinished. The theatre, high up on Monte Barbaro, has views out to Trapani and the sea and is still used for performances *(see p62)*. ® *1 km (2 miles) from Calatafimi • Map C3 • Open 9am- 1 hour before sunset • Adm.*

Lo Zingaro
5 Sicily's first nature reserve was instituted in 1980 to protect 7 km (4 miles) of rocky coastline on the Tyrrhenian Sea between Scopello and San Vito lo Capo. Marked trails of various levels of difficulty traverse the steep interior, or creep along the cliff above the sea, occasionally forking down to small coves with pebble beaches. The reserve protects flora and fauna such as wild orchids, limonium, wild carnations, dwarf palms, iris, remains of once widespread ilex and cork-oak forests, lichens and ferns, Bonelli's eagles, Peregrine falcons, Sicilian warblers, owls, porcupines and foxes. ® *Map B2*

Segesta

Around Sicily – Northwest Sicily

Marsala Wine

Marsala was "discovered" by John Woodhouse in the 18th century when he shipped some local wine to Liverpool, conserving it with added alcohol. The business took off, with Woodhouse, plus Englishmen Ingham and Whitaker and the Italian Florio fortifying wine purchased from peasant farmers. During the 20th century industrial versions gave it a reputation as a cooking wine, but since the 1970s producers have been working to produce high-quality Marsala once again.

6 Pantelleria

This tiny volcanic island, closer to Africa than Italy, is as well known for its VIP visitors as its natural beauty and culinary gifts. The architecture reflects Arabic influences and the island is dotted with *dammusi* – low, whitewashed, domed houses. Pantelleria is known for its caper production and the thick and sweet *moscato passito*, made from the native Zibbibo grape which grows well despite the *scirocco* winds. Map A6
• Hydrofoils: Siremar 0923 911 104, SNAV 0923-911 592 • Flights: Palermo and Trapani • Direct flights from Rome from 15 Jun–15 Sep

Pantelleria

7 Marsala

This sunbaked seaside town was founded in 397 BC as Lilybeo by Carthaginians fleeing Motya. It finally fell to the Romans after a 10-year siege, but it was the Arabs who named the city: Marsa Allah, meaning the port of God. Today, the town is best known as the landing point for Garibaldi's Redshirts *(see p37)* and for the wine that borrowed its name. The city survived successive invasions, but came into its own in the 18th century when the Marsala wine trade was born. The Baroque cathedral to San Tommaso di Canterbury presides over a pleasant piazza, where you'll also find the Museo degli Arazzi with its Renaissance tapestries from Madrid's Palacio Real (the gift of a Marsala-born archbishop).
 Map B3 • Museo degli Arazzi: piazza della Repubblica; Open 9am–1pm, 4–6pm Tue–Sun; Adm

8 Motya

This archaeological park occupies an entire island in Lo Stagnone, the lagoon north of Marsala, where the 8th-century BC Phoenician and later Carthaginian city thrived. Dionysus I of Syracuse destroyed Motya (Mozia in Italian) in 398 BC, leaving ruins of intricate fortifications, docks, homes decorated with mosaic flooring, and other structures. The extensive archaeological collections of the Museo Whitaker (former home of the English Marsala-producing family) are displayed as Whitaker intended – the highlight is the outstanding Greek marble statue of a youth in a diaphanous pleated tunic (c.440 BC). Map B3 • Museo Whitaker: Open 9am–1pm, 3pm-1 hour before sunset; Adm

Take advantage of free bikes in Marsala: tel. 0923 99 33 32.

Salt fields, Motya

9 Egadi Islands

Levanzo, Favignana and Marettimo are about 20 minutes from Trapani by hydrofoil and are great for relaxing on a summer's day as there is pretty much nothing here except for the sea. They are most famous for the *mattanza*, the Arabic tuna-fishing ritual that is still practiced here in spring. Favignana is dotted with tufa quarries that give the island a pockmarked look; the caves of Levanzo's interior have Paleolithic and Neolithic paintings, and swimming and sunbathing is good on all three islands. Marettimo, the furthest from the mainland, is known for its extraordinarily clear waters. *Map A3 • Hydrofoil and ferry: Trapani or Marsala*

10 Erice

On the top of a cliff above Trapani, ancient Eryx was known for its temple to Venus Erycina so large that it served as a beacon to sailors at sea. The temple was replaced with a castle in the Middle Ages, and the village, renovated at the same time, still has a medieval appearance. The main industry here is tourism and it feels like it, but it's a nice visit: local artisans make good ceramics and rugs, and the views are spectacular – on a clear day you can see all the way to Africa. *Map B2*

A Day Exploring Trapani

Morning

Start the day with a visit to Trapani's market in Piazza Mercato del Pesce. Well-stocked vendors are anxious to offer tastes of cheeses, olives and tuna. Pick out a few things for a picnic, then stop at the bakery on the corner of the piazza and via Torrearsa to round out your goodies with a *pane conzatu*, the sandwich you see the fishermen eating for breakfast. Walk down Via Torrearsa and pass under the arch into via delle Arti where Colicchia makes the best *cannoli* in Sicily *(see p71)*.

Follow via delle Arti to the piazzetta della Cuba and then via della Cuba down to piazza Notai. Take a look at Sant'Agostino church with its 14th-century rose window, before passing through the arch and back onto via Torrearsa. Going down Corso Vittorio Emanuele crane your neck to see the green majolica domes of San Lorenzo Cathedral, before reaching the end of the peninsula to enjoy your lunch and the sea views.

Afternoon

If you haven't spent all day shopping in Trapani, spend the afternoon up in **Erice**, with its good picnic sites and superb views. Or take the hydrofoil to the **Egadi Island** of Favignana.

Make it back to Trapani in time for the sunset to take part in the local *passeggiata*, then enjoy a wonderful traditional dinner at **Ai Lumi Tavernetta** *(see p97)*.

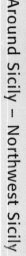

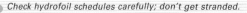

Left **Castelvetrano** Right **Baroque palace, Bagheria**

Top 10 Best of the Rest

1 Ossario di Pianto Romana
With sweeping views to the Golfo di Castellammare and Erice, an obelisk commemorates Garibaldi's defeat of Bourbon forces in May 1860 *(see p37)*. The victory allowed him to take Palermo, then all of Sicily, and eventually led to the Unification of Italy. ◎ *Map C2*

2 Castelvetrano
The "City of Olives and Temples", known for its olive oil production, can thank the Arabs for its urban plan and its central maze of piazzas. The bronze *Ephebus* (c.470 BC) is the pride of the Museo Civico. ◎ *Map B3*

3 Santissima Trinità di Delia
This splendid 12th-century Christian chapel mixes European, Arab and Norman styles. ◎ *Delia, 3.5 km (2 miles) from Castelvetrano.* • *Map B3* • *Closed to the public*

4 Bagheria
This village east of Palermo is now rather built up, but you can still see the elaborate Baroque villas built by Palermo's nobility, when it was all citrus groves and orchards. ◎ *Map D2*

5 Cusa Quarries
This natural quarry for Selinunte is located amid olive trees, with blocks of tufa and partially extracted columns. Slaves would have hauled columns 9 km (6 miles) to Selinunte. ◎ *Near Campobello di Mazara* • *Map B3*

6 Alcamo
This small village has a 14th-century castle of the Spanish Counts of Modica, who once ruled much of the region. It is best known for Bianco d'Alcamo, a white wine with DOC protection. ◎ *Map C2*

7 Marinella di Selinunte
The fishing village at Selinunte has a great morning market and a historic centre of fishermen's homes around the small port. The boardwalk is lined with bathing establishments, restaurants and bars. ◎ *Map C4*

8 Solunto
The Greek village of Solus was built on a grid plan in the 4th century BC, high above the sea. Lacking natural springs, it had a highly developed water conservation method. Among the ruins find cisterns, channels and pools. ◎ *Map D2*

9 San Vito lo Capo
On this dramatic promontory on the northwestern tip of Sicily is a resort with a long sandy beach and a promenade action-packed in summer. ◎ *Map B2*

10 Saline, Salt Pans
Exceptional sea salt is produced here using 16th-century windmills. The Museo delle Saline explains production *(see p54)*. ◎ *Map B2* • *Museo delle Saline: Salina Ettore e Infersa; Open 9:30am–6pm Sat–Sun; Adm*

Left **Belice Valley** Right **Castellammare beach**

TOP10 Landscape Features

1 Rolling Hillsides
The rolling hills of the Belice Valley are planted with wheat – green in winter, gold in summer, and burned black after the harvest – bordered by grape vines and olive trees. ◈ Map C3

2 Poggioreale Hill
On the road from old to new Poggioreale, a single wheat-covered hill rises up, topped with a lone wild pear tree. ◈ Map C3

3 Rugged Mountains
The rugged hills around Segesta, Calatafimi and Alcamo look dry and barren, but resourceful Sicilians plant them with hearty vines, cultivating the hills as high as possible. ◈ Map C3

4 Quarries
The rocky mountains between Trapani, Castellamare del Golfo and San Vito lo Capo are rich in marble, but are slowly being destroyed by huge industrial quarries extracting the stone for office buildings. ◈ Map B2

5 Faraglione
The rock towers at Scopello Tonnara jut out of the water, and are circled by seagulls who nest in the rocks' crevices. ◈ Map C2

6 Promontories
The enormous rocky formations hurled up by the sea include Monte San Giuliano (with Erice on top), Monte Cofano (with spectacular bays and a great view from Erice), and Monte Monaco at San Vito lo Capo. ◈ Map B2

7 Belice Valley
Near its mouth the wide, fertile Belice Valley is long, low, flat, and very good for farming; it's covered with a patchwork quilt of wine vineyards, olive groves, melon vines and citrus fruit trees. It is traversed by a typical Sicilian highway, raised on tall stilts.

8 Erosion
The Romans deforested Sicily to make way for profitable wheat farms. The result here is treeless earth, parched for much of the year and prone to drastic run-off during rains. When flooded with more water than they can handle, entire hillsides crumble into the sea.

9 Beaches
Long sandy beaches line the western coast of Sicily, reaching up to the huge stretch of sand at San Vito Lo Capo. Pebble beaches are found to the northwest, on the coast of the Golfo di Castellammare.

10 Plain
The mountains of the interior flatten as they near the sea toward Mazara, Marsala and up to Trapani on the northwest coast. The flat, sunbaked ground is fertile territory for grapes, olives and the salt pans.

Around Sicily – Northwest Sicily

Left **Cantine Florio** Right **Pina Parisi Tappeti**

⑩ Traditional Shops

❶ Pina Parisi Tappeti, Erice

Signora Parisi weaves exceptional rugs in geometric patterns and colours traditional to Erice. Her masterpieces, however, are rugs woven to her own designs, with naïve scenes of the Sicilian countryside, each signed with her initials, PP *(see p67)*. ✎ *Viale C.A. Pepoli 55 • Map B2*

❷ Perrone Ceramiche Souvenir, Trapani

In addition to ceramic plates, this family business produces traditional figurines of Sicilian peasants for nativity scenes and miniature terracotta replicas of traditional foods. ✎ *Corso Vittorio Emanuele 102 • Map B2*

❸ La Casa del Tonno, Favignana

The name, the House of Tuna, says it all. In the heart of Favignana, site of the *matanza (see p42)*, shop for canned tuna in oil and *bottarga* (dried tuna egg). ✎ *Via Roma 12 • Map A3*

❹ Altieri 1882, Erice

Since 1882 Altieri has been producing their own uniquely designed pieces in gold, coral and ceramics. ✎ *Via Cordici 14 • Map B2*

❺ Cantine Florio, Marsala

Inside the Florio institution is a nice store and a wine museum with a selection of antique tools used for wine-making. ✎ *Via Vincenzo Florio 1 • Map B3*

❻ Cantine Pellegrino, Marsala

This established Marsala family offers tours (in various languages) of the cellars and tastings. ✎ *Via del Fante 39 • Map B3*

❼ Alimentari Gerardi, Marsala

In this unusual grocer's there is a wide selection of prepared foods, cheeses and vegetables, and a great choice of wines. ✎ *Piazza G Mameli 11–14 • Map B3*

❽ La Bottega del Pane Rizzo, Castelvetrano

At his bakery, master baker Tomaso Rizzo uses Sicilian durum wheat or the ancient *tumminía* variety to make breads leavened with natural yeast and baked in an oven fired with olive branches. There are also the delicious *biscotti picanti* – biscuits made with black pepper and anise. ✎ *Via Garibaldi 85 • Map B3*

❾ Amaidda, San Vito lo Capo

A nice selection of Sicilian treats and wines – but they don't come cheap. ✎ *Via Savoia 83 • Map B2*

❿ Museo Saline, Trapani

The museum store sells boxes of traditionally produced sea salt. Sea salt has a rich flavour, which can vary, along with its saltiness, according to climatic conditions; the fine grain of the stone-ground salt adds texture to foods *(see p94)*.

Note: the Florio Museum and Cantine Pellegrino are only open by appointment.

Above **Osteria Il Mare il Colore del Vino**

🔟 Places to Eat

1 Ai Lumi Tavernetta, Trapani
A vaulted interior, tapestry placemats, modern paintings and antique implements. The menu has a few chosen Trapanese dishes and fresh fish *(see p77)*. ◈ *Corso Vittorio Emanuele 75 • Map B2 • 0923 87 21 18 • €€*

2 Pocho, San Vito lo Capo
Excellent cous cous served in an eclectic dining room with puppets hanging in the corners or on the breezy terrace looking down at Monte Cofano and the bay *(see p77)*. ◈ *Isulidda Makari • Map B2 • 0923 97 25 25 • Closed Tue, winter • €€*

3 La Crapraria, Scopello
This extra-small shop sells fantastic sandwiches on delicious breads. Try *pane cunsatu* with tomatoes, cheese, oregano, salt, pepper, olive oil, and sardines – a heavenly bite of Sicily. ◈ *The Piazza • Map C2 • No credit cards • €*

4 Da Peppe, Trapani
Near the port, Peppe cooks up Trapanese dishes, fresh fish and excellent stuffed calamari (squid). ◈ *Via Spalti 50 • Map B2 • 0923 28 246 • Closed Mon, winter • €€*

5 La Bettola, Favignana
There is no menu here, just a selection of whatever fish was caught that day and a few vegetable dishes. A good place to be in spring when the tuna are running. ◈ *Via Nicotera 47 • Map A3 • 0923 92 19 88 • Dis. access • €*

6 Il Vignetto, Menfi
In countryside covered with vineyards, eat out under a pergola, choosing from a seasonal menu – Sicilian tagliatelle with wild fennel, fava beans and ricotta, for example, with local wines. ◈ *Contrada Gura del Mare • Map C3 • 0925 71 732 • Closed Sun D, Mon winter • €€*

7 Osteria Il Mare il Colore del Vino, Marsala
Behind a bright yellow façade find modern art, ceiling fans and a summer menu of snacks, salads and seafood, all designed to accompany the Sicilian wines. ◈ *Via Caturca 13 • Map B3 • 0923 71 95 31 • Closed Tue, winter • €*

8 La Pineta, Selinunte
Expertly prepared, extremely fresh fish served on the beach under torchlight. ◈ *Via Marinella • Map B4 • 0924 46 820 • €€€*

9 Ruvido, Marsala
A new restaurant with creative, fresh dishes based on either fish or meat. A mix of Sicilian and mainland Italian traditions. ◈ *Lungomare Mediterraneo 27 • Map B3 • 0923 71 97 44 • €€*

10 Taverna del Pavone, Monreale
A selection of Sicilian favourites with an emphasis on Palermitan specialities in a cozy interior, a stone's throw from the cathedral. ◈ *Vicolo Pensato 18 • Map C2 • 091 640 6209 • Closed Mon • €*

Note: *Unless otherwise stated, all restaurants accept credit cards and serve vegetarian meals*

Left **Mount Etna** Right **Giardini Naxos**

Northeast Sicily

THE NORTHEAST OF SICILY CAN'T HELP BUT BE DOMINATED *by Mount Etna*, although the region also consists of three mountain ranges, a group of islands with another active volcano, and two of Sicily's largest cities. Parts of this area have been devastated by wars, earthquakes, tidal waves and lava flows, but the land and the people that live on it come back after each ordeal, heartier and more steadfast. Perhaps that is why people here celebrate feast days of their patron saints with so much fervour. High up in the hills and peaks of the Nebrodi and Madonie mountains, it often seems like nothing has changed for eons – the same castles that safeguarded the royal passageways of the interior now stand guard over modern *autostrada*.

Sights

1. Aeolian Islands
2. Taormina
3. Mount Etna
4. Cefalù
5. Catania
6. Giardini-Naxos
7. Messina
8. Straits of Messina
9. Madonie Mountains
10. Tindari

Giardini Pubblico, Taormina

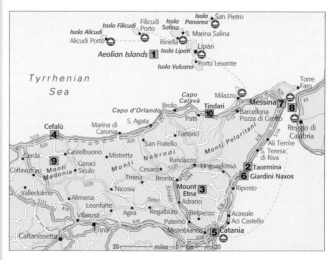

1 Aeolian Islands

The islands were declared a World Heritage Site by UNESCO in recognition of the ongoing evolution of the volcanic forms that creates their spectacular scenery. The islands remain an important study area for vulcanologists (see pp12–13).

2 Taormina

Sicily's first true holiday resort has been drawing visitors for centuries, all of whom fall in love with its sparkling, colourful beauty (see pp14–15).

3 Mount Etna

Europe's largest active volcano dominates Sicily – from much of the island it is rarely out of sight and never out of mind (see pp16–17).

4 Cefalù

This small fishing village, now a resort thanks to its good sandy beaches, lies on a strip of land between the sea and a huge promontory looming above. Cefalù was founded in the 4th century BC, but destroyed by the Norman Count Roger in 1063. It only regained prominence thanks to his son Roger II, who endowed the village with a bishopric and a church decorated with exceptional Byzantine mosaics. The modern holiday

Cefalù waterfront

Duomo, Catania

resorts lie to either side of the town because the village itself has closed its doors to the sea, fortified itself against storms with tall protective stone walls, and focuses its attentions inwards (see p101). ◈ Map E2

5 Catania

Sicily's second largest city has had its unhappy share of earthquakes and volcanic eruptions, and although Catania is rich in monuments dating back to its Greek foundations, the city seen today was built mostly after the massive 1693 earthquake. The rebuilding was largely carried out in the elaborate Baroque style, utilizing the workable local black lava stone. The most important monuments are grouped around the Piazza Duomo with the 1736 Elephant Fountain, the Duomo itself, dedicated to Sant' Agata and retaining its original Norman apses, the Fish Market in via Garibaldi (see p67), the Roman theatre, the castle (see p47), via Crociferi with its Baroque palaces, and via Etnea with its shops and cafés. ◈ Map G4

From Ice to Ice Cream

Greeks and Romans used Mount Etna's snowfall to chill their wine, and the Arabs, bringing with them sugar and citrus, used it to make cold, sweet drinks. Sicilian chefs were long accustomed to combining ice with sugar and natural flavours (lemon, jasmine, cinnamon) to make *granite* and sorbet, but by the beginning of the 1700s, whether they invented the concept or borrowed it from their mainland neighbours, they had perfected the craft of ice cream-making, adding to their repertoire the chocolate brought by the Spanish from the New World. Sicilian *gelato* is now famous the world over *(see p71)*.

6 Giardini-Naxos

According to ancient historians Naxos was founded in 734 BC after a ship was blown off course as it sailed to southern Italy, and it became the first Greek settlement in Sicily. Naxos never became a powerhouse but was mother city to successive colonies and the setting off point for messengers carrying news back to Greece. The ruins, defensive walls and parts of a temple are enclosed within a nicely kept park. A small museum houses finds from the Greek site, as well as finds recovered from shipwrecks. ◈ *Map H3 • Museum: Open 9am–4pm daily • Adm*

7 Messina

Founded by colonists from Messenia, Greece, the city grew up around the harbour, which has always been its focus. In 1908 Messina was levelled by a disastrous earthquake and tidal wave, although parts of the older city survive. Monuments are concentrated around the magnificent harbour, including the Norman Duomo with original portals and sculpture, a 15th-century fountain in the Piazza Duomo and a clock tower whose mechanized figures come to life at noon, the Santissima Annunziata dei Catalani with its Norman features, the 1572 monument to Don Giovanni of Austria, and the Museo Regionale, with important works by Antonello da Messina *(see p60)* and Caravaggio. ◈ *Map H2*

8 Straits of Messina

The narrow strait between Messina and Reggio di Calabria was supposedly guarded by Scylla and Charybdis, the mythical sea creatures who led sailors astray. A proposed suspension bridge linking Sicily and mainland Italy has been under debate for more than 30 years. Sicilians are split between those who believe a link to the mainland would open up Sicily to much-needed economic development, and those who fear a loss of their insularity, and thus autonomy. Many suggest that the island infrastructure should be addressed first – much of Sicily still lacks basic necessities such as decent roads and water and electricity supplies. ◈ *Map H2*

Duomo and view of Messina

Madonie Mountains

9 Madonie Mountains

The Madonie range, featuring Sicily's highest peaks after Mount Etna, extends from Cefalù inland and is protected by the Parco Naturale Regionale delle Madonie. The park encompasses spectacular countryside, forests of beech, chestnuts, cork oaks, poplars and fir, and tiny villages that time seems to have forgotten. The remote villages that once provided refuge to bandits on the run are now good starting points for mountain hikes, horseback riding, cycling and skiing *(see pp52–3)*. 🌐 Map E3

10 Tindari

The extensive ruins of ancient Tyndaris, first Greek and then Roman, lie to either side of the Decumanus Maximus, the main street. Homes show mosaic flooring, drainage and the remains of heating systems. A restored basilica with graceful arches spans the street where it marked the entrance into the public area. A theatre, built by the Greeks, modified by the Romans and still in use, was sited to take advantage of the view out to sea. A small museum houses finds from the site including a colossal head of Augustus. Nearby visit the sanctuary of the Black Madonna, a pilgrimage favourite. 🌐 Map G2

A Morning Walk Around Cefalù

🕐 Start your walk at Piazza Garibaldi, beginning at Corso Ruggiero, where the church of Santa Maria della Catena is built on top of the 5th-century BC town walls. Walking down the Corso, on the left at the corner of via Amendola is one of the only extant parts of Norman Cefalù, besides the cathedral, the Palazzo Osterio Magno. Pass the flower-filled piazzetta in front of the Chiesa del Purgatorio on your way to Piazza Duomo, which opens up to the right. Inside the **cathedral** *(see p44)* admire the mosaics, but don't miss the exterior view of the apse around the back. Sit out in the piazza at Bar Duomo with a *cappuccino* and enjoy the cathedral façade and the church bells marking the hour.

Continue down the Corso to the end, take a left on via Bordonaro and a right into Piazza Crispi with views of the Greek walls later absorbed by Spanish fortifications. Follow via Bordonaro down to Piazza Marina with the small port below. Off to the left, down the via Vittorio Emanuele, a staircase leads to *lavatoi* (washbasins), the sole remnant of Arab domination.

Before lunch, enjoy a wander around the "real" Cefalù, where fishermen repair boats and women pause from their laundry to chat.

🍴 Have lunch in the garden at L'Antica Corte *(Corso Ruggero 193 • 0921 423 228)* or pick up picnic supplies from Alimentari e Salumeria Gatta Gaetano *(Corso Ruggero 152)*.

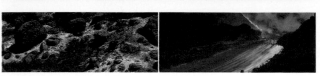

Left **Sulphur emissions** Right **Lava flow**

🔟 Mount Etna Eruptions

1 693 BC
A massive eruption destroyed the Greek settlement at Katane (ancient Catania).

2 396 BC
Lava flows from this eruption reached the Ionian Sea, preventing the Carthaginian Himilco from landing and thus stopping him from marching on Syracuse.

3 1169, 1329 and 1381
Eruptions in these three years sent lava all the way to the sea. The first arrived at Aci Castello; the last flowed all the way to Catania, pouring into the sea at Ognina and covering the Portus Ulixis, mentioned by Virgil in the epic poem *The Aeneid*.

4 1669
The worst eruption in modern times was preceded by three days of earthquakes. On the third day, a crevice 14 km (8.5 miles) long opened from the summit to Nicolosi and disgorged quantities of ash, rocks and lava. The eruption lasted four months, destroying several towns and leaving 27,000 people homeless.

5 1886
Lava flows from this eruption once again threatened the village of Nicolosi, but the veil of St Agatha was carried in a procession and the lava miraculously stopped. It was not the first time that St Agatha had purportedly halted a lava flow.

6 1911
Two major eruptions on the north side created a 5-km (3-mile) long crevice and 170 temporary craters. This crevice opened up again in 1923.

7 1928
A huge eruption destroyed the town of Mascali and a significant amount of cultivated land and buildings. It is the only time during the 20th century that a village was destroyed.

8 1979
An explosion killed nine tourists who were on the edge of the main crater, then poured lava into the Valle del Bove and almost reached Fornazzo.

9 1991–93
During these eruptions lava flowed down the Valle del Bove towards Zafferana Etnea, prompting authorities to try to divert the flow with explosives and by dropping concrete blocks from helicopters. The lava stopped just 1 km (half a mile) from the village.

10 2001
Called the most complex eruption in 300 years, Etna disgorged ash and lava from six openings on the north and southeast sides, destroying the Etna Sud cable car station, threatening the Rifugio Sapienza and causing officials periodically to close roads and Catania airport.

For details on the 2002 eruption See p17

Left **Boating** Right **Horse riding**

🔟 Outdoor Activities

1 Hiking, Madonie
The Madonie mountains are crisscrossed with marked trails graded for difficulty; several trails are suitable for the disabled. The trail map is available from the park service, tourist offices of larger towns within the park system, or from the tourist office in Palermo. The Italian Alpine Club organizes guided excursions.
⚲ *Italian Alpine Club: 091 62 54 352*

2 Horse Riding, Madonie
The trails of the Madonie can be used by horse riders too. Several groups arrange trips.
⚲ *Ranch San Guglielmo: Castelbuono, 0921 67 11 60 • Rifugio Francesco Crispi: Cactolbuono 0921 67 22 79*

3 Hiking, Aeolian Islands
You can hike up the slopes to Vulcano's crater following the signs *al cratere*. Take a guide from the hydrofoil dock up the active volcano Stromboli.

4 Swimming, Aeolian Islands
Good swimming abounds in the Aeolians – the water is clear and rich in marine life.

5 Boating, Aeolian Islands
The best way to visit hidden coves and grottoes, and the only way to get from island to island, is by boat. From Marina Corta in Lipari take your pick from a wide selection of organized tours. For experienced sailors, boat rentals are available. ⚲ *Private Boat Tours: Bartolo Greco, 090 98 11 347*

6 Walking, Tindari
Below the promontory, from Capo Tindari towards Oliveri and Falcone, the Tindari-Oliveri reserve is good for a quiet walk along the sand formations and lakes with blue-green water.

7 Hiking, Nebrodi
The Nebrodi Mountain Park encompasses protected yew and beech woods, pastureland, a wetlands habitat for migratory birds, birds of prey and wild horses. The park includes 21 villages where artisans produce local goods and food. Marked trails are available for hiking.

8 Alcantara Gorge
The Alcantara River runs at the bottom of a 20-m (65-ft) deep basalt gorge. From the car park, with waders for rent, walk down the steps or take the lift to the bottom, where you can hike between the narrow walls and over waterfalls.

9 Hiking, Mount Etna
Ascend towards the main crater or hike the slopes accompanied by a guide. ⚲ *Gruppo Guide Alpine Etna Sud: 095 791 47 55 • Gruppo Guide Alpine Etna Nord: 095 647 833*

10 Skiing, Mount Etna
There are about 10 ski runs on Etna. Lift tickets and equipment rentals are available.
⚲ *South Etna Ski School: Nicolosi, 095 78 00 739 • Star: 095 643 430 • Stel: 095 643 814*

⮕ *Note: after heavy rainfall the water level of the Alcantara Gorge can be dangerously high.*

Left **Mount Etna souvenirs** Right **Designer boutiques**

🔟 Specialist Shops and Markets

1 Mount Etna Souvenirs
The best in lava kitsch can be had at the base of Etna Sud or Etna Nord. Ashtrays, mini statues of San Pio, turtles – you name it, it has been moulded from molten lava and dipped in blue glitter. There are also more subdued trinkets, literature and videos of eruptions. ◐ *Map G3*

2 A Puttia Perivancu, Viagrande
Since 1926 this shop has offered the best of local wild fruits and greens, cheese, bread, pistachios, mushrooms, marmalade and wine. ◐ *Via Bellini 18 • Map G3*

3 Markets
Small street markets spring up in villages on Mount Etna's slopes. Local farmers offer their produce for sale from their cars and three-wheeled pick-up trucks, many near Fleri, between Viagrande and Santa Venerina.

4 Via Entea, Catania
This district is famed for big-name Italian stores such as Max Mara, Benetton, Rinascente, Frette, as well as inviting pastry shops and cafés. Emporio Armani and other designer boutiques continue on the Corso Italia. ◐ *Map G4*

5 Le Colonne, Taormina
The proprietor of this jewellery store in Taormina creates pieces from old stones, inspired by historical motifs; she

also works on commission if you create your own design. ◐ *Corso Umberto I, 164 • Map H3*

6 Parisi, Taormina
Here you'll find the top names in classic Italian high fashion, including Prada, Dolce & Gabbana, Ferre and Armani. ◐ *Corso Umberto I, 46 • Map H3*

7 Ceramiche dell'Artigianato Siciliano di Managò, Taormina
Signore Managò's Sicilian ceramics include traditional designs from Caltagirone and Santo Stefano di Camastra. ◐ *Via S Domenico 1–2 • Map H3*

8 F.lli Laise Delizie Eoliane, Lipari
This store's booty of Aeolian goods includes capers of every kind, sweet sundried tomatoes, honey, oregano and wine. ◐ *Via Vittorio Emanuele 118 • Map G1*

9 Il Sandalo, Lipari
You choose the style of heel and pick your own straps, and the artisans in this store will make custom-made sandals of wood and leather. All you have to do is come back later to pick them up. ◐ *Via Maurolico 2 • Map G1*

🔟 Ceramiche Josa, Santo Stefano di Camastra
This shop produces examples of Santo Stefano's famous orange-and-yellow ceramics. ◐ *Via Nazionale 104 • Map F2*

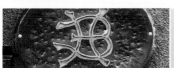

Above **Hostaria Bellini**

Price Categories

For a three-course meal for one with half a bottle of wine (or equivalent meal), taxes and extra charges.

€ under €25
€€ €25–€35
€€€ €35–€55
€€€€ €55–€70
€€€€€ over €70

🔟 Places to Eat

1 Ristorante Mulinazzo, Mulinazzo

This is the place for creative versions of traditional Sicilian dishes, all to be enjoyed in a beautiful dining setting. There's a good wine list, too. ® *Contrada Mulinazzo 121 • Map G3 • 091 872 4870 • Closed Sun D, Mon • €€€*

2 Il Cuciniera, Catania

Devoted to the cuisine of Ragusa, Syracuse and Catania, this restaurant focuses on high-quality local produce. The wine list offers more than 20 labels from the Etna region alone. ® *Katane Palace Hotel, via Finocchiaro Aprile 110 • Map G4 • 095 74 70 702 • Dis. access • €€*

3 Ristorante Gangivecchio, Gangivecchio

In this former Benedictine monastery, set deep within the Madonie Park, you can sample savoury mountain specialities made with local rabbit, lamb and pork, all served with fresh vegetables from the proprietors' farm. ® *Outside Gangi • Map E3 • 0921 68 91 91 • Closed Mon • €*

4 Ristorante Nenzyna, Lipari

This tiny *trattoria* near the port has a bright blue façade and pavement tables. The owner is a grandmother who has been preparing the menu of fresh fish and other Aeolian Island favourites for more than 40 years. ® *Via Roma 4 • Map G1 • 090 981 1660 • Dis. access • €*

5 Trattoria da Pina, Vulcano

Good Aeolian cuisine is served on a dockside terrace at Gelso, with views all the way to Mount Etna. ® *Gelso • Map G1 • 368 66 85 55 • No credit cards • €*

6 La Grotta, Acireale

An actual grotto, this tiny restaurant is a favourite of locals, who proclaim the excellence of the fish. ® *Via Scalo Grande 46 • Map G3 • 095 76 48 153 • Closed Tue • Dis. access • €€*

7 Osteria Antica Marina, Catania

This *osteria* near the fish market sells a selection of each day's catch. Try the marinated anchovies. ® *Via Pardo 29 • Map G4 • 095 34 81 97 • Closed Wed • Dis. access • €*

8 A Zammará, Taormina

The menu offers Sicilian dishes eaten in a garden of orange trees or in the quaint arched dining room. ® *Cia Filli Bandiera 15 • Map H3 • 0942 24 408 • Closed Wed in winter • €€€*

9 Ristorante Pizzeria Granduca, Taormina

This terraced pizzeria has wonderful views. ® *Corso Umberto 170 • Map H3 • 0942 249 83 • €*

10 Hostaria Bellini, Adrano

A perfect little *trattoria*. Try the spicy aubergine (eggplant) pasta. ® *Vicolo Platania 34 • Map G3 • 095 769 1555 • Closed Mon • Dis. access • €*

Around Sicily – Northeast Sicily

Note: Unless otherwise stated, all restaurants accept credit cards and serve vegetarian meals

Left **Prizzi, Il Corleonese** Right **Palazzo Adriano, Il Corleonese**

Southwest Sicily

THE BEAUTY OF SOUTHWEST SICILY *lies even beyond the splendid mosaics of the Villa Romana and the temples at Agrigento. Sandy beaches, lovely fishing villages, ruined Greek cities and silvery olive and dark green citrus groves feature all along the little-developed coastline. Enna dominates the wide, wheat-filled valleys, while small farming villages of the unspoiled interior remain isolated on their hilltops, with vast expanses of rocky mountains or rolling fields between them. Because of the lack of infrastructure, the area remained remote until well into the 19th century, then mass emigration slowed modern development in the 20th century. As a result, these little villages have remained almost as they were centuries ago, a testimony to Sicily's agrarian past.*

🔟 Sights

1. Villa Romana del Casale
2. Agrigento and the Valle dei Templi
3. Il Corleonese
4. Sciacca
5. Enna
6. Caltabellotta
7. Morgantina
8. Eraclea Minoa
9. Badia di Santo Spirito, Caltanissetta
10. Pelagie Islands

Morgantina

1 Villa Romana del Casale
The finest surviving Roman mosaics in the world cover the floors of this official's luxurious hunting villa *(see pp24–5)*.

2 Agrigento and the Valle dei Templi
The Valley of the Temples was the heart of one of the most important cities in the ancient world and is a prime example of the magnificence of Magna Graecia *(see pp26–9)*.

3 Il Corleonese
The central zone around the village of Corleone *(see p49)* is referred to as *il Corleonese* and has long been known for its generous water supplies and fertile soil – driving through the countryside, the richness of the land is evident. Small, remote villages are sprinkled throughout, all worth a quick visit to witness a way of life that is slow to change. Among them, visit Prizzi, Bisacquino, Palazzo Adriano, Cammarata, Mussomeli and Corleone itself, a successful modern town with a lovely historic centre. ✪ *Map C3*

4 Sciacca
Dominated by Monte San Calogero and built on a terrace over the sea, this was the thermal spa town for Selinunte and still has a spa offering restorative sulphur and mud baths. The small port town has an interesting harbour choked with little blue-and-white boats, a thriving ceramics tradition and a good mix of old and new. See the Porta San Salvatore (1581) carved by local artisans with carpet-like decorative reliefs, and the Catalan-Gothic Palazzo Steripinto with its diamond-shaped rustication. Then walk the

Palazzo Steripinto, Sciacca

Corso Vittorio Emanuele to the Piazza A Scandaliato for views down to the port, then on to the Duomo for its Baroque façade with Gagini sculptures. ✪ *Map C4*

5 Enna
Because of its easily defendable position on the top of a tall hill, Enna was almost the only town in the interior for centuries. The Greeks called it the "umbilicus of Sicily", and it was a key position for any group that wanted to take the island. Enna was so well defended that the Arabs, having tried to capture it for 20 years, resorted to crawling in through the sewer system. In the historic centre see the Gothic Duomo with Baroque renovations; the church of San Giovanni with an Arab dome; the Museo Alessi's comprehensive ancient coin collection and objects from the Duomo's treasury; and the museum of Sicily in Miniature, documenting local traditions, such as costumes from Holy Week festivals. ✪ *Map E4 • Museo Alessi: Enna Cathedral; Open 9am–1pm Tue–Sun; Adm • La Sicilia delle Miniature e della Musica: via Roma 533; Open 9am–1pm Tue–Sun; Adm*

6 Caltabellotta

This tiny village, 950 m (3,100 ft) above sea level, has a lovely medieval centre. In 1090, the already fortified village was taken from the Arabs by the Norman king Count Roger, who built the Chiesa Madre and fortified the now ruined castle. It was in this castle in 1194 that William III, heir to the Norman throne, and his mother were imprisoned and probably murdered by Emperor Henry VI; it was also the site of the signing of the 1302 peace treaty between Frederick II of Aragón and Charles of Valois, putting an end to the Sicilian Vespers *(see p36)*. ✪ *Map C4*

7 Morgantina

Morgantina was settled first by the Italic Morganti people, then by the Greeks in the 6th century BC, then the Romans, but it was only excavated in 1955. The extensive, well preserved site comprises a split-level *agora* (forum) connected by a 14-step staircase that served as the site of town meetings, the *macellum* (covered market), a gymnasium, a public fountain with a double basin, large black

Cliff, Eraclea Minoa

lava millstones, residences with mosaic flooring, a 1,000-seat theatre, an enormous public granary and kilns for firing terracotta.The larger of the two kilns was also used for firing construction materials. ✪ *Map F4* • *Open 9am–1 hour before sunset daily* • *Free*

8 Eraclea Minoa

Above vineyards and olive groves thriving in the rocky soil and on the white sandstone cliffs, the ruins of this ancient Greek city lie on a headland above a wide sandy beach. Midway between Selinunte and Agrigento and on the border between Carthaginian- and Greek-held territory, Eraclea Minoa saw its fair share of border disputes. The site is quiet now, and well kept. A small museum and groomed paths lead to an intimate theatre carved into the sandstone, remains of defensive walls with towers and the residential section where a few houses made of local stone preserve their floor and wall decorations. Since it's not on the standard tour bus route, the added pleasure of a visit is that you may have this gorgeous place all to yourself. ✪ *Map C4* • *Open 9am–7pm daily* • *Adm*

Oranges and Other Citrus Fruits

Citrus fruits were introduced to Sicily by the Arabs and have been an important cash crop for centuries. There are lemons, both sharp and sweet, tangerines, mandarins and endless varieties of oranges, from sweet to sour, from pale gold to dark purple. The plantations, plentiful particularly in the zone around Ribera, are characteristic for their low-growing trees with dark green leaves, bright fruits and heady fragrance (la zagara).

9 Badia di Santo Spirito, Caltanissetta

The Abbey of the Holy Spirit was founded around 1090 by Count Roger and his wife, Adelasia, and consecrated in 1153. It is one of the few Romanesque Norman buildings to remain intact. The exterior is unadorned except for the portals and the small, triple apse articulated with tall, narrow arcading. The interior contains 14th- and 15th-century frescoes and an dedicatory inscription dating from 1153 in the apse.
◎ *Badia • Map E4 • Open 9am–noon, 4–6pm daily • Free*

10 Pelagie Islands

The three flat islands that form this group are romantically isolated in the middle of the Mediterranean. Lampione is uninhabited, while Linosa is known for its fertile, volcanic soil and crystal clear waters. Lampedusa, the largest of the three at 20 sq km (7.5 sq miles), responded to a tourism boom with modern buildings, but is still good for swimming, diving and watching sea turtles, dolphins and whales (they migrate in March). The coast of Lampedusa was the object of the 1987 Libyan missile strike that fell short, dumping missiles into the sea. ◎ *Map B6*

Lampedusa, Pelagie Islands

An Afternoon in Caltabellotta

🕐 Take a late afternoon drive from Sciacca up to **Caltabellotta**. Skip the modern outskirts of town to wander around the narrow streets and piazzettas of Terravecchia, the old medieval centre. Terravecchia lies on a flat plain under the Chiesa Madre founded by Count Roger one year before he took Palermo *(see pp8–9)*. It's newly restored, so admire the entry portal with pointed arch and the bell tower which was originally an old Arabic fortification; inside see the *Madonna of the Chain, St Benedict* and *Madonna and Child* – all works by the artist Gagini.

To the north of the church take the little path up the rock to the ruins of the Castelvecchio, the old castle, from which you can look down on Caltabellotta and out over the valley.

On the other side of the plain, opposite the Chiesa Madre, find the tiny church of San Salvatore with its zig-zag decoration around the door. Use the steps carved out of the rock to climb up to the highest point of Monte Castello. Walk around the ruins of Count Roger's castle, with its single Gothic doorway, and take in one of the most stunning views in Sicily. To the southwest see the coastline from **Agrigento** *(see pp26–9)* to **Marsala** *(see p92)*.

Back in town, stroll from Piazza Umberto I to via Roma in the newer part of the village, where you can have an excellent dinner of mountain fare at the **Trattoria Ferla** *(see p115)*.

 You can get to the Pelagie Islands by flying from Palermo or taking a ferry from Porto Empedocle.

Left **Sicilian citrus fruits** Right **Ceramics**

Local Produce

1 Wine
During the 20th century large estates planted with wheat and other crops started planting vines to produce high-quality wine. Two examples are Regaleali near Vallelunga and Planeta near Sambuca di Siclia.

2 Co-operative Produce
In and around Corleone *(see p49)*, several co-operatives under the umbrella *Libera Terra* cultivate land confiscated from mafia bosses to create jobs and strengthen the economy of the area. Wheat is grown for pasta, grapes for wine, as well as fruits, cheeses and honey.

3 Oranges
Ribera is known for its production of the prized Washington variety of navel orange, introduced to the area by emigrants returning from North America.

4 Crude Oil
In 1954 crude oil was discovered off the coast of Gela. An offshore platform, port and jetty were built, and within a decade Gela was equipped with a petro-chemical plant for refining domestic and imported oil.

5 Sulphur
Natural sulphur deposits from Agrigento to Caltanissetta were exploited by the owners of *latifondi* (large farms) underneath whose land the deposits lay. Sicilian sulphur mining was infamously inefficient, using child labour, primitive extraction and mules until well into the 20th century, thereby selling sulphur at double the market price.

6 Fresh Fish
Fishing villages line the southern coast of Sicily with important centres at Licata, Porto Empedocle and Sciacca.

7 Preserved Fish
Preserved tuna was a staple food for centuries on ships sailing the Mediterranean, and tuna as well as anchovies and sardines are still big business. At Sciacca, anchovies and sardines are processed by hand and packed under salt or olive oil for export all over the world.

8 Wheat
The interior of the island was taken up with *latifondi* until well into the 20th century and it's still an important source of income. Vast valleys and hills are devoted to cultivating Sicily's special *grano duro (see p70)*.

9 Ceramics
Traditional ceramics are still made in various centres, notably Sciacca where the designs are in green, yellow and blue.

10 Fava Beans
Large fava beans are cultivated in the countryside near Enna. They are eaten dressed with olive oil or used in soups.

Left **Prizzi** Right **Enna Valley**

🔟 Scenic Views

1 From Caltabellota
From the ruins of the Norman castle above Caltabellota *(see p110)* you can see all the way to the flat coast stretching toward Marsala and the hilly interior dotted with villages and farms. *Map C4*

2 The Valle dei Templi by Night
Agrigento's temples are even more romantic at night. You can see them from any vantage point but perhaps the finest view is from the terrace at Il Dehors *(see p115)*, enjoying an excellent meal with the Temple of Concord as backdrop *(see pp26–9)*.

3 Prizzi
Driving through the Corleonese zone *(see p109)*, Prizzi is one of the highest towns, covering the top of its hill like a *cobbola* (peasant farmer's cap). *Map D3*

4 Views from Enna
From the Piazza Cripsi see across the deep valley to Calascibetta on the flat top of its own terraced hill, and across the interior all the way to Mount Etna. *Map E4*

5 Enna
From the valley floor to the east, Enna presents an impressive sight, the Rock of Demeter dominating the cliff above the site where Persephone was abducted by Hades *(see p109)*.

6 Countryside around Corleone and Prizzi
Vast expanses of rolling terrain are planted with wheat, vines, olives and silvery blue artichokes. Colours pop up here and there amid the green, such as a large swathe of crimson sulla, bright red poppies and hearty yellow fennel growing impossibly tall *(see p109)*.

7 Vallate near Enna
The enormous *vallate* (valleys) around Enna are planted with wheat, and the spectacular stretches of soft fields change colour with the seasons, from lush green, to golden yellow, to black. *Map E4*

8 The Rocca di Nadore
The round-topped Rocca di Nadore above Sciacca turns its flat, white face towards the sea and dominates the coast for miles. See it looming on the horizon as far away as Selinunte. *Map C4*

9 From Morgantina
From the residential sector on the east hill, look down on the *agora* (forum) and out towards the east coast and the outline of Mount Etna *(see p110)*.

10 From Eraclea Minoa
From the ruins of Eraclea Minoa on top of a white sandstone cliff, look down to the wide stretch of sandy beach and the dark sea *(see p110)*.

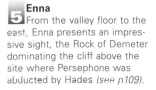

Around Sicily – Southwest Sicily

Left **Lago di Pergusa** Right **Enna**

TOP 10 Chthonic Deities and their Sites

1 Demeter
The cult of the Mother Goddess, protectress of agriculture and fertility, is one of the most ancient in Sicily. When her daughter Persephone disappeared, Demeter roamed the Earth searching for her, ignoring crops, and thus allowing the earth to become wrought with famine.

2 Persephone
The daughter of Demeter and Zeus (also known as Kore or, to the Romans, Proserpine) rules as both Queen of the Underworld and Goddess of Fertility.

3 Persephone's Abduction
While gathering lilies, violets and hyacinths with her girlfriends in fields below Enna, Persephone was abducted by Hades and taken to reign as Queen of the Underworld.

4 Persephone's Return to Earth
Hades agreed to release Persephone on condition that she ate a pomegranate seed (food of the dead) so ensuring her return to the Underworld for four months each year. When she reigns in the Underworld, it is winter on Earth; when she returns, she brings spring and renewal.

5 Lago di Pergusa
A deep natural lake south of Enna is the supposed site of the passage from Earth to the Underworld.

6 Sanctuary at Enna
The seat of the cult of Demeter and Persephone was at Enna on the boulder behind the castle. Their temple contained a statue of the Mother Goddess.

7 Votive Offerings from the Sanctuary at Enna
Items recovered from the sanctuary and from sites near Lake Pergusa are preserved in Enna's Museo Archeologico, including votive statuettes of Demeter. ◈ *Museo Archeologico, Palazzo Varisano, Piazza Mazzini • Map E4 • Open 9am–6:30pm daily • Adm*

8 Rock Sanctuary of Demeter, Agrigento
The earth goddesses were venerated at a sanctuary now marked by the church of San Biagio. The church was built on top of a 5th-century BC temple; two round altars are extant *(see p27)*.

9 Sanctuary at Morgantina
Demeter and Persephone were worshipped as the protectresses of Morgantina. In the sanctuary see purification baths, altars for performing rituals and a well for sacred offerings.

10 Sanctuary at Palma di Montechiaro
Three 7th-century BC votive statuettes of Demeter or Persephone, now in Syracuse's archaeological museum, were recovered from this sanctuary between Agrigento and Gela.

Price Categories

For a three course meal for one with half a bottle of wine (or equivalent meal), taxes and extra charges.

€ under €25
€€ €25–€35
€€€ €35–€55
€€€€ €55–€70
€€€€€ over €70

Above **Il Dehor de l'Hotel Foresteria Baglio della Luna**

TOP10 Places to Eat

1 Il Dehor de l'Hotel Foresteria Baglio della Luna, Agrigento

The chef prepares local foods with an international flair in an elegant, quiet and friendly dining room *(see p77)*. Ⓝ *Valle dei Templi, contrada Maddalusa* • Map D4 • 0922 51 10 61 • *Dis. access* • €€

2 Ristorante Pomara, San Michele di Ganzaria

The restaurant centres around the stone fireplace where local cheeses, vegetables and meats are grilled to accompany hearty dishes such as pasta with pistachios. Ⓝ *Via Vittorio Veneto 84* • Map F4 • 0933 978 032 • *Dis. access* • €

3 La Ferla, Caltabellotta

A local favourite, now in a new, larger space with a terrace and sea views. Try the roasted artichokes and local cheeses. Ⓝ *Via Roma 29* • Map C4 • 0925 951 444 • *Closed Mon* • *Dis. access* • €

4 Ruga Reale, Agrigento

A casual *osteria*, frequented by locals. Under large arches and wooden beams or on the terrace sample a small menu of fish and meat dishes. Ⓝ *Piazza Pirandello 9 (cortile Scribani)* • Map D4 • 0922 20 370 • *Closed Wed* • *Dis. access* • €

5 Hosteria al Vicolo, Sciacca

A large menu made up of fantastic combinations of local ingredients, including lots of fish. Ⓝ *Vicolo Sammaritano 10* • Map C4 • 0925 23 071 • *Closed Mon* • €€

6 Acquarius, Santo Stefano Quisquina

Hearty foods of the interior, including lamb, pork ribs and carefully selected local sausage, cheese and wines. Ⓝ *Via Libero Attardi 62* • Map D3 • 0922 982 432 • *Closed Wed* • €€

7 Civiletto, Sutera

A country restaurant set in a former monastery with tasty, hearty fare, including wood oven-baked bread, local cheeses and olive oil. Ⓝ *Via San Giuseppe 7* • Map D4 • 0034 954 587 • *Closed Mon* • €

8 Il Paiolo, Bisacquino

A large restaurant that draws locals for its simple, good food, such as fresh fava beans (in season) and grilled local sausage. Ⓝ *Via Decano di Vincente 97* • Map C3 • 091 835 1036 • *Closed Mon* • *No credit cards* • *Dis. access* • €

9 Trattoria dei Templi, Agrigento

This family-run *trattoria* has a reputation for its Sicilian menu: try the pasta with swordfish and mint. Ⓝ *Via Panoramica dei Templi 15* • Map D4 • 0922 403 110 • *Closed Jul–Aug: Fri & Sun* • €€

10 La Giarra, Corleone

A local favourite, with an outdoor terrace in summer. Local cheeses, meats and vegetables and live music and dancing on Saturday and Sunday nights. Ⓝ *Contrada Belvedere* • Map C3 • 091 846 4964 • *Closed Mon* • *Dis. access* • €

Note: Unless otherwise stated, all restaurants accept credit cards and serve vegetarian meals

Left **Palazzolo Acreide** Right **Noto beach**

Southeast Sicily

THE LANDSCAPE OF THE SOUTHEAST IS MARKEDLY DIFFERENT *from the rest of the island, with its strata of white limestone supporting scrubland vegetation, steep gorges formed by ancient river courses, and characteristic low, dry-stone walls marking the boundaries of fertile fields. Yet this small corner of Sicily is rich in sights. Unmissable are the Greek and Roman remains at Syracuse, the most important city of Magna Graecia, while Caltagirone, Modica, Noto, Palazzolo Acreide, Ragusa and Scicli have all recently been declared World Heritage Sites on the merits of their Baroque architecture and innovative urban planning, the result of the rebuilding effort after the destruction of the 1693 earthquake. Of*

equal enjoyment is the current gastronomic renaissance taking place in the area, rediscovering both the seafood from the coastal zones and the meats, cheeses and wild greens of the interior. Young chefs, aware that old traditions, methods and even ingredients are on the brink of extinction, are returning to their roots and working hard to revitalize and preserve the authentic cuisine of the region.

San Domenico, Noto

Sights

1	Syracuse
2	Noto
3	Ragusa Ibla
4	Modica
5	Scicli
6	Palazzolo Acreide
7	Southeast Plains
8	Caltagirone
9	Grammichele
10	Pantalica Necropolis

1 Syracuse
Remains of the mighty powerhouse of Magna Graecia make up some of the most important sites in Sicily, while the small historic centre of Ortygia *(see p124)* is one of the most pleasant town centres on the island *(see pp18–21)*.

2 Noto
Noto is the chief proponent of the new cities built entirely in Baroque style after the 1693 earthquake destroyed most of eastern Sicily. Noto was rebuilt using a tufa stone that has turned a golden shade after years of sun, while the architecture is ebullient and dramatic. The town plan involves open, wide streets with plenty of piazzas and piazzettas for gathering and making the *passeggiata (see pp22–3)*.

3 Ragusa Ibla
Ragusa was founded as Hybla Heraia by Siculi peoples fleeing inland to escape the Greeks. After the earthquake of 1693, half the population chose to rebuild on the ridge above, (Ragusa) while the other half

Ragusa Ibla

chose to renovate the old village, (Ragusa Ibla). Ibla makes an immediate impression with its little terracotta roof-tiled buildings clinging dramatically to the side of a cliff. The Duomo is at the heart of town, sited on a rise to emphasize its great height. A Gagliardi masterpiece of 1744, the façade is articulated with a pulsating entablature, bulging columns and swirling volutes pushing upwards toward the tall central bell tower. The oval-shaped cathedral of San Giuseppe presents another projecting Baroque façade. Also not to be missed is the surviving portal of the pre-quake cathedral, Catalan-Gothic in style and with a delicately carved St George slaying the dragon. Map F5

4 Modica
Rebuilt after 1693, on and between two deep gorges, the city is dramatically divided in two parts – Modica Alta, the upper town, and Modica Bassa, the lower town. Founded by the Siculi, the city attained great importance under Spanish rule when it was the capital of a quasi-autonomous state ruled by Spanish barons. The lively Corso Umberto I, with boutiques, cafés, pastry shops, numerous palaces and a theatre, crosses Modica Bassa. Also on this street is a monumental flight of steps with excellent Baroque statues of the Apostles that leads up to the post-1693 Duomo dedicated to San Pietro. Up the hill, Modica Alta's Baroque church of San Giorgio is attributed to Gagliardi. Inside there is characteristic stucco work and 10 beautiful 16th-century wooden panels depicting scenes from the New Testament. Map G6

5 Scicli

Dominated by a high, rocky cliff, Scicli was an outpost of the Spanish barons during their long reign over the County of Modica. From the wide Piazza Italia, the via Nazionale leads up to the west, passing the side street where the Palazzo Beneventano sits on a corner, its sculptural decoration now weathered by the elements. Via Nazionale continues to the pleasant Piazza Busacca with views down into the older, residential section of town with its narrow lanes and crumbling terracotta roofs. ◈ *Map F6*

6 Palazzolo Acreide

The "modern" Baroque town was originally a Greek colony of Syracuse, founded in 664 BC. At the archaeological site just next to the village, the small, 600-seat Greek theatre remains in good condition, although temples to Persephone and Aphrodite are in ruins. Old quarries bear a Greek banqueting scene and a Roman sacrifice carved in relief. A short walk outside the old city are the *Santoni* (Big Saints), enormous statues of fertility goddess Cybele and her entourage carved out of the rock *(see p49)*. ◈ *Map G5*

Carob Trees

Enormous *carrubi* (carob trees) are a characteristic feature of southeast Sicily. The trees produce a fruit shaped like a brown pea pod, with sweet flesh and small, hard seeds. The seeds are amazingly uniform and were the original karat used to weigh precious stones. Carob's sweet flesh can be used in pasta and sweets. Once called "poor man's chocolate" the deep, rich flavour is now prized by the best chefs of the region.

Caltagirone

7 Southeast Plains

On the upland plain around Ragusa and Modica the soil is marked with white stone outcroppings and gorges, while on the lowland plain around Vittoria, the tufa lies almost 1 m (3 ft) below the surface and is topped with a layer of red soil that supports bright green grapevines. Pastures criss-crossed with walls are marked by stone *masserie* (farmer's homes). The farmer *(massaro)* works the fields, raises livestock and produces grain, olive oil and milk for the local *caciocavallo Ragusano* cheese.

8 Caltagirone

Named after the Arabic *Cal'at Ghiran* (Castle of Vases), ceramic production has been the main industry in this town since prehistoric times, a tradition documented at the local Museo della Ceramica. The Baroque town built onto a steep hillside is a pleasure to wander through, with characteristic alleyways, cafés and ceramics shops. A stairway leads from the lower town up to the church of Santa Maria del Monte, and each of the 142 steps is decorated with majolica tiles. ◈ *Map F4*

In Scicli have a coffee on the terrace at Pura Follia on Via Nazionale, looking out at the tiled rooftops of the old village.

9 Grammichele

Built by the Principe di Butera after the 1693 earthquake to house the farmers of the destroyed village of Occhiolà, this lovely place preserves an authentic peasant-farmer feel, even though it was built on a grand plan inspired by Renaissance mathematical ideals. The concentric hexagonal plan radiates from around the central Piazza Umberto I, home to private residences, *palazzi*, the Chiesa Madre and the town hall. ⬡ *Map F5*

10 Pantalica Necropolis

Pantalica was at the heart of ancient Hybla, the culture known now only through its striking red glazed pottery, examples of which are on view in Syracuse. The Anapo River carved a steep gorge through the limestone creating what became Sicily's largest necropolis; there are more than 8,000 tombs here. A hike through the gorge takes you past thousands of burial sites, carved into the cliff sides, as well as remains of a medieval settlement, wild orchids, irises, rabbits, porcupines, falcons, trout and crabs. ⬡ *Map G5*

Pantalica Necropolis

A Day in Modica and Ragusa Ibla

Morning

🕐 Spend a morning in **Modica** *(see p117)*, stopping by the church of San Giorgio of Modica Alta on your way into town. In Modica Bassa, visit the **Museo Iblea delle Arti e Tradizioni Popolari SA Guastella** *(see p123)* with its excellent collection displayed in recreated homes and craftsmen's workshops. Walk down the Corso Umberto I towards the Duomo, passing cafés, shops and buildings that incorporate parts of pre-earthquake structures. At Corso Umberto I, 156, visit the *biscottificio* of Donna Elvira Roccasalva for a taste of Modica's traditional sweets.

Drive along the SS 115 to **Ragusa Ibla** *(see p117)* crossing one of the tallest viaducts in Europe into a fertile land of citrus groves and carob trees. In via Capitano Bocchieri pick up a map of the maze-like streets from the information office. Next door, have lunch at **Ristorante Duomo** *(see p125)*.

Afternoon

Spend the afternoon wandering through Ragusa Ibla to see the Duomo, San Giuseppe and San Giorgio Vecchio. You can study the Baroque façade of the Duomo from under the trees in the lively piazza with a treat from Gelati DiVini *(Piazza Duomo 20)* – their ice cream is made from Sicilian wines. But don't fail to walk through the narrow side streets where tiny alleys are connected with staircases and tunnels, for a taste of authentic Ibla.

Left **Castello di Eurialo** Right **Villa Natalina, Modica**

TOP 10 Best of the Rest

1 Noto Antica
To the northwest of Noto lie the evocative ruins of the pre-earthquake town. Built on an arid, limestone ridge, the site commands views of the Ragusan plain and Mount Etna. Under the hot Sicilian sun, purple thistle and sundried herbs perfume the air. ◈ *Map G5*

2 Castello di Eurialo
This Greek military castle was built in 402 BC and is notable for its 15-m (50-ft) keep. Spectacular views of the coastline can be had from its fortifications *(see p46)*. ◈ *Map G5 • Open 9am–1 hour before sunset • Free*

3 Giarratana
This tiny town in the middle of the Monte Iblei has narrow streets lined with palaces, churches and residences. Note the typical homes, with low doors, to protect against cold winter winds. ◈ *Map G5*

4 Olympieion
Built in the 6th century BC and set amid cypress trees, two of the temple's 42 columns remain standing. ◈ *Map G5*

5 Ciane River
The river's source is a pool formed by the tears of Cyane, who tried to prevent Persephone's abduction into the underworld. The river banks are thick with papyrus. Take a boat tour past the Olympieion. ◈ *Map G5*

6 Vendicari
The reserve's *maquis* supports thyme, rosemary and juniper; the wetlands host migratory birds. Depending on the season, watch for herons, egrets and flamingoes. ◈ *Map G6*

7 Cave d'Ispica
An ancient river carved out this gorge, which is now an open-air park with good walks and climbs. The cliff sides are hollowed out to form ancient tombs and cells of religious hermits; in one of the caves is a Byzantine fresco of the Madonna. ◈ *Map G6 • Open 9am–6pm daily • Free*

8 Marzamemi
This little fishing village grew up around the *tonnara* (tuna fishery) and villa of the noble Villadorata family. The old village remains, but with the addition of modern resort features including popular nightclubs. ◈ *Map G6*

9 Summer Houses of the Nobility
The wealthy families of Modica built elaborate summer homes in the countryside. Drives lead to walled villas with grand façades, courtyards and elegant gardens.

10 Villa Rizzone, Modica
This Neo-Classical 19th-century villa has an open courtyard planted with palms, while the interior is painted in blue and gold. ◈ *Map G6 • Closed to the public*

Left **Casa Museo di Antonino Uccello** Right **Museo Iblea delle Arti e Tradizioni Popolari**

Ethnographic Museums

1 Museo Iblea delle Arti e Tradizioni Popolari SA Guastella, Modica

Here, rooms from a peasant's home, artisans' workshops and laboratories are faithfully recreated. See typical workshops of the blacksmith, basketmaker, shoemaker, cartmaker, and a complete pastry workshop with original utensils. ® *Map G6 • Open 10am–1pm, 4–7pm daily • Adm*

2 Villa-Museo Cozzu zu Cola, Floridia

Materials here have been collected from *masserie* (farmer's homes) throughout the Iblean countryside. They include mills for wheat and olives, looms and a large collection of handmade tools. ® *Near Syracuse • Map G5 • Open 11am–1pm, 4–6pm daily • Adm*

3 Casa Museo di Antonino Uccello, Palazzolo Acreide

Among the exhibits of Sicilian tradition here are puppets, decorated carts and work room and living quarters of a peasant home *(see p39).* ® *Via Machiavelli 19 • Map G5 • Open 9am–1pm, 3:30–7pm daily • Adm*

4 Museo del Macino del Grano, Palazzolo Acreide

An antique water-powered grain mill has been restored and put back into action, complete with the mill stones that grind wheat into flour for bread and pasta. ® *Map G5 • Open 9am–1pm, 3:30–7pm daily • Adm*

5 Centro Documentazione della Vita Popolare Iblea

The centre preserves 120 hours of film and 6,000 prints documenting work in the fields and the cycles of agricultural life. ® *Buscemi, via Vittorio Emanuele • Map G5 • Open by appt only • Adm*

6 I Luoghi del Lavoro Contadino, Buscemi

This tiny village is now a living museum, where eight work rooms and living spaces have been faithfully preserved. They include the home of a peasant farmer, a smithy, olive press and a water-powered mill. ® *Map G5 • 0931 878 528 (call to arrange a tour)*

7 U parmientu, Buscemi

The grape press here has intricate workings handmade in wood and stone.

8 U trapplitu, Buscemi

The olive press is housed in a space hewn out of the rock.

9 A casa ro massaru, Buscemi

The peasant farmer's home has a kitchen complete with wood-burning stove.

10 A casa ro iurnataru, Buscemi

The day labourer's house is a poorly furnished space of 12 sq m (130 sq ft). It was inhabited by six people until the 1960s, illustrating social conditions of the Sicilian countryside.

Full day tours of Buscemi include lunch and a visit to the Museo del Macino del Grano.

Around Sicily – Southeast Sicily

Left **Ortygia market** Right **Temple of Apollo**

⏀ Ortygia Sights

1 Ortygia
The tiny island is a bustling mix of temples, churches, museums, open piazzas, seaside bars, markets and shops.

2 Temple of Apollo
On Largo XXV Luglio are the remains of the Doric Temple of Apollo. Built in 575 BC, this was the first temple in Sicily with an exterior colonnade of stone columns. Two monolithic sandstone columns remain.

3 Piazza del Duomo
Excavations here turned up remains of the 8th-century BC houses of the original Sicel culture. Around the oblong piazza are the Duomo, the town hall (located atop an Ionic Temple to Artemis) and outdoor cafés.

4 Duomo
One of the most spectacular buildings in Sicily, the dramatic Baroque façade fronts a 5th-century BC Doric Temple to Athena. It was transformed into a church in the 7th century AD. Clearly visible inside and out are monolithic Doric columns.

5 Galleria Regionale del Palazzo Bellomo
The 13th-century Palazzo Bellomo houses the fine arts museum. The star features are Caravaggio's *Burial of St Lucy* and Antonello da Messina's *Annunciation*. ✆ *Via Capodieci 16 • Open 9am–1:30pm Mon–Sat, 9am–12:30pm Sun • Adm*

6 Fonte Aretusa
The mythical Arethusa *(see p37)* was turned into a spring and bubbles up on the shores of lower Ortygia. Along the Lungomare Alfeo a little terrace looks down on the spring that now feeds into a pond, with ducks and tall papyrus.

7 The Greek Ghetto
The six parallel streets between via della Giudecca and via GB Alagona follow the Greek urban plan. It is still crowded with medieval houses and laundry flapping in the breeze.

8 Castello Maniace
Frederick II built this castle around 1239. It takes its name from the Byzantine George Maniakes who "liberated" Syracuse from the Arabs in the 11th century. Not open to the public.

9 Market
The market typically bustles with local housewives and vendors yelling out the merits of their wares. Farmers and fishermen heap mussels, tomatoes, cherries or whatever is plentiful into colourful mounds to entice customers. ✆ *Via Giaraca & via Trento • Mon–Sat am*

10 Via Maestranza
Now lined with boutiques and restaurants, this street was where noble families built their Baroque palaces, often incorporating older structures.

Enjoy the sunset from the Alfeo Bar on the Lungomare at the Fonte Aretusa.

Above **Don Camillo**

Price Categories	
For a three-course meal for one with half a bottle of wine (or equivalent meal), taxes and extra charges.	€ under €25
	€€ €25–€35
	€€€ €35–€55
	€€€€ €55–€70
	€€€€€ over €70

🔟 Places to Eat

1 Ristorante Duomo, Ragusa Ibla

Ciccio Sultano expertly chooses and prepares local ingredients. The food is outstanding, served in an elegant dining room *(see p76)*. ⊗ *Via Capitano Bocchieri 31 • Map F5 • 0932 65 12 65 • Closed Mon • €€€*

2 Locanda del Borgo, Rosolini

In a restored castle with original frescoes and red drapery, traditional techniques are revisited to create innovative dishes *(see p76)*. ⊗ *Via Controscieri 11 • Map G6 • 0931 85 05 14 • Dis. access • €€€*

3 Ristorante Fidone Maria, Friginitini

This family-run place near Ragusa prepares everything in house, and it's all excellent *(see p76)*. ⊗ *Via Gianforma Margione 10 • Map F5 • 0932 90 11 35 • Dis. access • No credit cards • Closed Mon • €*

4 Gargantua, Modica

Only five tables in a barrel-vaulted space in old Modica, where the chef prepares local, seasonal foods. ⊗ *Corso Umberto 261 • Map G6 • 0932 75 29 27 • Closed Sun D & Mon • €€*

5 Eremo della Giubiliana, Ragusa Ibla

Traditional Ragusan recipes are prepared with vegetables from the estate's garden, and bread and pasta from their own wheat. ⊗ *Contrada Giubiliana • Map F5 • 0932 66 91 19 • Dis. access • €*

6 Sakalleo, Scoglitti

The menu depends upon what the owner's fishing boats bring in. The animated owner may also have a glass of wine with you. ⊗ *Piazza Cavour 12 • Map F5 • 0932 87 16 88 • Dis. access • €€*

7 Da Majore, Chiaramonte Gulfi

"Qui si magnifica il porco" ("Here the pig is glorified") is the motto of this restaurant, which is also a butcher's. ⊗ *Via Martiri Ungheresi 12 • Map F5 • 0932 92 80 19 • Closed Mon • €*

8 Al Molo, Donnalucata

Sit on a terrace facing the wharf where fishermen sell their catch under brightly striped awnings. Fish is prepared simply or in more elaborate Sicilian dishes such as sweet and sour stingray ⊗ *Via Perello 90 • Map F6 • 0932 93 77 10 • Closed Mon • €€*

9 Don Camillo, Syracuse

Typical Syracusan dishes served in a pretty interior with arched brick ceilings. ⊗ *Via Maestranza 96 • Map H5 • 0931 67 133 • Closed Sun • €€*

10 Trattoria La Foglia, Syracuse

Eat well in this quirky restaurant where opera blasts out of the speakers, menus are hand-decorated in fake luxurious fabrics, and the decor is homely. ⊗ *Via Capodieci 21 • Map H5 • 0931 66 233 • Closed Tue • €€*

→ **Note:** Unless otherwise stated, all restaurants accept credit cards and serve vegetarian meals

STREETSMART

SICILY'S TOP 10

Left **Crowded summer street scene** Centre **Tourist office sign** Right **Beach in summer**

10 General Information

1 When to Go
With temperature in mind, the best times to visit are May, June, September and October. Every season is beautiful, even winter, when bright green shoots of wheat start to sprout and you can ski on Mount Etna. Summer is lovely, but it can get very hot in July and August, and the beaches are crowded.

2 What to Pack
With a wealth of activities available, pack accordingly: if you're heading for Etna, take a good map, sturdy hiking shoes, a torch and a warm coat; if it's a beach destination, you'll need sunglasses, swimming gear, sandals for pebble beaches, sun protection and a beach towel.

3 Tourist Offices Abroad
Ente Nazionale Italiano per il Turismo is the national Italian tourist board and has offices in numerous countries. Check the website for your home country.
ⓘ www.enit.it • USA: 30 Fifth Avenue, Suite 1565, New York, NY 10111; (212) 245 5095 • UK: 1 Princes St, London W1R 8AY; (020) 7408 1254

4 Tourist Offices in Sicily
Tourist offices in Sicily are randomly staffed and randomly open, but it is worth stopping in for

information on local exhibitions, concerts, plays and listings of bars, restaurants and entertainment. Look for the signs with an "i" on a yellow background.

5 Embassies and Consulates
Foreign embassies are mainly located in Rome, but there is a US consulate in Palermo (the British Consulate in Palermo offers no services). ⓘ US Consulate: Via Vaccarini1, Palermo • 091 305857 • www.usembassy.it

6 Passports and Visas
Non-EU citizens must present a valid passport to enter Italy; EU members only need an identity card. Visas are not necessary for citizens of the EU, USA, Canada, Australia or New Zealand for stays of less than three months. Other nationalities should check with their embassies. Apply for visas in person and well in advance at the Italian embassy or consular office in your home country.

7 Customs
EU residents are not charged duty on goods purchased in Italy, although certain limits may apply. US citizens are allowed to bring in up to $400 worth of goods before customs duties are applied. No fruits,

vegetables, meats, fresh cheeses or farm products can be brought in.

8 Public Holidays
Shops, post offices and banks close on public holidays (see box).

9 Electricity and Water
Electrical current is 220V, and plugs have two or three round prongs. Sicily is notorious for poor electrical and water supplies – periods of drought are frequent. Small inland towns have the most problems, but hotels are well equipped. Everyone drinks bottled water although tap water is usually potable.

10 Opening Hours
Opening hours for shops vary between 8:30am and 10am. Nearly everything closes for lunch at 12:30pm until 2:30pm or even 3:30pm.

Public Holidays

Epiphany
6 Jan

San Giuseppe
19 Mar

Liberation Day
25 Apr

Labour Day
1 May

Ferragosto
15 Aug

All Saints' Day
1 Nov

Whether you are hiking or spending a day at the beach, it's always advisable to carry a bottle of water.

Left **Fontanarossa Airport, Catania** Right **Punta Rais Airport, Palermo**

🔟 Getting to Sicily

1 By Air from Europe
Some carriers provide direct flights to Sicily during the summer season. Out of season there are no direct flights and it is necessary to make a connection at a mainland Italian airport, picking up flights with Alitalia or Meridiana.

2 By Air from the Americas
There are no direct flights into Sicily from American airports. Flights from the Americas to Italy generally land in Milan or Rome, where connections can be made into Palermo or Catania.

3 By Air from Australia
Again, there are no direct flights to Sicily. Fly into a major mainland Italian airport such as Milan or Rome and make a connection to one of the Sicilian airports.

4 Palermo Airport, Punta Rais
Tiny Palermo airport is equipped with a bank and car rental companies. It is located west of Palermo, about 40 minutes from the centre and an hour or so from Trapani or Castelvetrano. Prestia e Comandè runs a bus service between Punta Rais and the centre every half hour, with stops at the airport, the Piazza Politeama and the central train station.

5 Catania Airport, Fontanarossa
Convenient for the eastern side of the island and just 20 minutes from Catania's centre, tiny Fontanarossa is also equipped with a bank and car rental companies. The airport buses (Alibus) leave every 20 minutes stopping at the airport, via Etenea and the central train station.

6 Domestic Airports
Palermo and Catania may be small but they are the largest airports in Sicily. Charter flights may take advantage of smaller airports such as Birgi at Trapani. There are also airports on Pantelleria and Lampedusa serving flights from Trapani and Palermo

7 By Train
Trains from mainland Italy are loaded onto boats and ferried across the straits of Messina, calling at Messina before making their way south to Catania or west to Palermo. Check with your travel agent for times and fares or directly with the Italian State Railway. 🖑 *Italian State Railway: Ferrovie dello Stato • 020 7724 001 • www.trenitalia.it*

8 By Car
If you want to travel in your own car rather than renting one on the island, you can take a *traghetto* (ferry) to Sicily from Genoa, Livorno, Naples or Reggio di Calabria in southern Italy. From Reggio or nearby San Giovanni, take FS, Caronte or Meridiano across the Straits of Messina to Messina itself (30 minutes). Grandi Navi Veloci takes 20 hours from Genoa to Palermo or 18 hours from Livorno to Palermo. Tirrenia sails from Naples to Palermo in 16 hours. Siremar sails from Naples to the Aeolian Islands and Milazzo in 11 hours. 🖑 *Tirrenia Navigazione: Naples: 081 251 47 21; www.Tirrenia.it • SNAV, Naples: 081 761 23 48; www.snavali.com • Grandi Navi Veloci, Genoa: 010 55 091; www.gnv.it • Siremar, Naples: 081 761 36 88; www.siremar.com*

9 By Boat
Ferry details are the same as if travelling by car, but if you are on foot you can take a much faster *aliscafo* (hydrofoil), with service offered by the same companies.

10 By Private Plane
If you're flying your own plane, land at any of the numerous small-craft airports (the website below has details) or choose the private airfield at Giubiliana near Ragusa. 🖑 *AOPA Italy: Aeroporto Milano Bresso 20091 Bresso, Milan; 02 665 01485; aopa.italia@ aopa.it; www.aopa.it • www.accukwik.com (for lists of airports)*

Left **City bus transport** Right **Travelling by scooter**

Getting Around Sicily

1 By Car

It is easiest to get around Sicily by car, particularly in the remote interior. Bring a good map, an international driving licence, and all the necessary paperwork for your vehicle as the Italian authorities spend a good deal of time examining documents. Beware of city traffic: the fast-moving pace, impatient Italian drivers and narrow, one-way streets can be nervewracking. In Palermo and Catania it is best to park the car and explore by bus and on foot. ✆ *Roadside assistance: 116.*

2 Car Rental

Car rental is available at major airports and in cities and larger towns. Most companies do not charge a drop-off fee if you remain on the island, so you can pick a car up in Palermo and drop it off in Catania for no extra charge. Several private companies rent cars on the offshore islands.

3 Road Rules

Sicily's reputation for aggressive drivers may seem deserved at first glance but if you look closely, you'll notice that everybody lets everyone else cut in. Make eye contact, take advantage of an opening, and merge. There are, of course, people who just ignore all the rules, so always stay alert.

4 City Public Transport

Bus service in cities and large towns is reliable and extensive, and a good way for tourists to get around. Tickets are available from kiosks near major stops, from some bars and from tobacconists (look for the black sign with a "T"). Validate your ticket in the yellow punch card machine once on board.

5 By Train

Train services, provided by the Italian State Railways *(Ferrovie dello Stato)* do exist in Sicily, but with more routes available in the eastern part of the island than in the west. Timetables are available on the Internet *(see p129)* or pick one up at a station. The main train station in town is called the *stazione centrale*. Service is reliable for the most part but trains can run late.

6 By Bus

Bus services are comprehensive and heavily used by Sicilians, who often work or attend school or university away from their home village. A variety of regional bus companies provide coverage throughout the island (reduced service on Sundays). The main bus companies are SAIS, Interbus and AST. Bus stations are called *auto-stazione* and are usually located near train stations.

7 By Bicycle

If you are an experienced cyclist Sicily offers some good biking opportunities but beware of the long distances and steep inclines. Bicycles are for rent in cities and on the offshore islands, for very reasonable rates if not for free *(see p53).*

8 By Boat

Ferries *(traghetti)* and hydrofoils *(aliscafi)* ply the routes between Sicily and the offshore islands, ports on mainland Italy, as well as Sardinia and Corsica *(see p129).* Private boats, with a captain if you prefer, are available for rent from many ports, and fishermen are usually willing to give tourists a quick tour.

9 By Scooter

Scooter rentals are reasonably priced and a fun way to get around smaller towns and the offshore islands. Rental companies provide helmets, instructions and usually a map. It is not recommended for big city transport as the traffic is chaotic and truly dangerous for scooters.

10 Taxi

Taxis are available in cities from marked taxi stands and work on a metered basis. Taxi drivers are also open to setting a fee for a day or more of a private service if you want to get around without driving yourself.

If driving in Sicily, watch out for stop signs that are often painted directly on the road rather than overhead on road signs.

Left **Escorted tour of Selinunte** Right **Horse riding in the Madonie Mountains**

🔟 Specialist Holidays

1 Food tours
Peggy Markel's Culinary Adventures offer a food-orientated tour of Palermo, Ragusa, Modica, Noto, Syracuse and Taormina, staying in 4- and 5-star accommodation. For small group tours of Sicily with a dual culinary and cultural focus, Esperienze Italiane's staff will organize an itinerary providing experiences with leading chefs, wine estates and art historians. 🖎 *Peggy Markel's Culinary Adventures: PO Box 54, Boulder, CO 80306, USA; (303) 440 8598; www.cookinitaly.com • Esperienze Italiane: 243 E 58th St, New York, NY 10022, USA; (212) 758 1488; shelly@lidiasitaly.com*

2 Italian Language
The Babilonia language school in Taormina holds courses of between five and ten people, offered at various levels, with oral and written communication as the goal. Courses range from two weeks to six months. Housing is provided and a wide variety of cultural programmes and trips is included. 🖎 *Babilonia Centro di Lingua e Cultura Italiana: via del Ginnasio 20, Taormina • 0942 23441 • www.babilonia.it*

3 Senior Citizen Holidays
Elderhostel offers educational tours emphasizing art, archaeology and history for travellers aged 55 and over. Two Sicily tours cover the island with a good selection of sites, including some off the beaten track. Lectures by specialists give an insight into the culture with additional topics such as cuisine and the Mafia. 🖎 *Elderhostel: 11 Avenue de Lafayette, Boston, MA 02111, USA • (877) 426 8056 (within US & Canada); (978) 323 4141 (from outside US & Canada) • www.elderhostel.org*

4 Day Trips and Activities
Actividayz offers a wide variety of day trips and hands-on activities – hike Etna with a geologist, visit a pistachio farm, meet a puppet-maker in his workshop, or visit a ceramic factory and decorate your own vase. English-speaking guides. 🖎 *The Parker Company: 152 Lynnway, Lynn, MA 01902, USA • (781) 596 8282 • www.actividayz.com*

5 Hiking
Country Walkers offers hiking trips with English-speaking guides and 4- and 5-star accommodation. Ramblers Holidays offers walking tours of Etna, Ancient Sicily and the Aeolian Islands. 🖎 *Country Walkers: PO Box 180, Waterbury, VT 05676, USA; (802) 244 5661; www.countrywalkers.com • Ramblers Holidays: PO Box 43, Welwyn Garden City, AL8 6PQ, UK; 01707 331133; www.ramblersholidays.co.uk*

6 Yachting and Sailing
Seven Seas Yacht Charter offers power boat and sailboat charters, with or without a crew. 🖎 *Seven Seas Yacht Charter: 2216 Lakeshore Drive, Nokomis, FL 33427, USA • (941) 966 6017 • www.visailing.com*

7 Horse Riding
Horse riding is available through *agriturismi* (see p53) and through agencies in the Nebrodi and Madonie mountains. For details, call the park offices. 🖎 *Parco Regionale delle Madonie: 0921 684 011; apm@abies.it • Parco Regionale dei Nebrodi: 0921 333 211; parconebrodi@legacyl.it*

8 Cooking Schools
Anna Tasca Lanza teaches Sicilian cooking and provides accommodation at her wine estate, Regaleali. 🖎 *www.cuisineinternational.com*

9 Escorted Tours
Caravellaltalia's "Ancient Sicily" is a comprehensive escorted tour of the island with luxury accommodation. 🖎 *Caravellaltalia: 2112 Walnut St, Philadelphia, PA 19103 USA • (215) 665 1233 • www.seeitaly.com*

10 Package Tours
All-inclusive package tours are available from Orizzonti, which also has a selection of properties on the offshore islands. 🖎 *www.orizzonti.it*

Left **Driving on a narrow Sicilian street** Right **Mountain snake**

10 Things to Avoid

1 Tourist Meals
A fixed-price meal can be a good deal, but avoid tourist meals offering generic Italian "specialities" such as *pasta alla'bolognese*, *spaghetti alla carbonara*, or anything with a cream sauce. Your best bet is simple foods prepared with high-quality and fresh Sicilian ingredients.

2 The Mafia
The Mafia does not bother tourists and it's highly unlikely that you would run into anything connected to the group. Sicilians are more comfortable now about speaking out against Mafia violence, however, although they are generous with advice and directions, they remain suspicious of anyone asking too many questions.

3 Snakes
Be on the look-out for snakes in the mountains or sunning themselves on the ancient stones of archaeological sites. For the most part they are not poisonous and slither off as soon as disturbed, but it's a good idea to wear shoes and socks instead of sandals when clambering around ruins.

4 Chemical Plants
Sadly, not all of Sicily's coastline is pristine. Particularly east of Palermo, near Milazzo, between Catania and Syracuse, and near Gela, there are enormous petro-chemical plants, usually marked with signs saying *agglomerato industriale* and belching pollution into the air and sea water.

5 Large Cars
If you're driving, don't rent a car larger than you need. In big cities it will be hard to park, and in small towns and villages it will be hard to squeeze through narrow city gates or tiny streets designed to bear nothing wider than a mule-drawn cart. It helps to look ahead for vehicles to ensure the street is transitable – some village roads narrow until they turn into footpaths or become so steep they turn into staircases.

6 Dressing Inappropriately
Not every church enforces the proper dress rule, but they can if they want to. Short shorts are not appreciated, and nor are skimpy tops with bare shoulders. Simply covering your shoulders with a scarf or a makeshift shawl usually solves the problem.

7 Backtracking
Sicily is deceptively large. Avoid backtracking over great distances to catch your flight home. Fly into Palermo and out of Catania or vice versa.

8 Wild Fires
Lack of rain and the broiling sun make Sicily very dry in summer and wild fires are common. Do your best not to set them off by extinguishing cigarettes properly and not lighting campfires unless it is expressly allowed. If you see a fire, call the Bosco (Forest) Hotline on 115. If you are near a fire, try to stay up wind and follow the instructions of the *Vigili del Fuoco* (firemen).

9 Theft
You're no more prone to thieves in Sicily than anywhere else in Italy, but use general common sense. Lock your car, don't leave any items exposed (including the radio if you have that option), keep an eye on your wallet and backpack in crowded places, don't flaunt jewellery, use caution at ATMs, and don't leave valuables unattended on the beach.

10 Scams
Market stalls putting on the hard sell don't always have the freshest goods. Beware especially in Palermo's Vucciria market, where some vendors may rip you off. Beware also of the expensive *"giro d'isola"* tour of the island, offered by taxi services on the offshore islands. Unless you want the full tour, make sure the meter is running or set your price in advance.

Left **Food products to take home** Right **Wine shop**

🔟 Shopping Tips

Opening Hours
1 Most shops are open from 8:30 or 9am–1pm and from 3:30–7:30pm, with some variation; they are required to post their hours on the door. In tourist areas in summer shops stay open during lunch. Shops that keep Saturday hours often stay closed one day during the week. Stores selling clothing and gift items are closed on Monday mornings, and food shops close on Wednesday afternoons.

How to Pay
2 Credit cards and travellers' cheques are not as widely accepted or appreciated as cash. You'll also get a discount for paying in cash on occasion (or pay slightly more for a credit card transaction).

Tax Refunds
3 Value added tax (IVA) is included in the price of goods for sale in stores. Non-EU citizens can get the tax refunded if they spend more than €150 in any one store. The salesperson will provide and fill out the paperwork. You have three months to file the forms with the Tax Free office in the airport of your last EU stop. You must provide the forms, receipts and sometimes produce the goods. Refunds are provided on your credit card or in cash on the spot.

Ceramics
4 Artisan ceramic production in Sicily is of good quality. Traditional styles vary from area to area and some craftsmen produce good modern designs as well. Examine each piece carefully to make sure there are no gaps in the glaze. You might be able to bargain for a discount on a slightly flawed piece. If you want the ceramics posted home, most stores are adept at packing and shipping, but make sure insurance is included or they have an arrangement with their courier service.

Haggling
5 Haggling is common in markets for any items except food, which is so reasonably priced that you won't need to haggle anyway. Shops do not haggle over prices unless something is flawed, but if you spend a lot in a particular store, it never hurts to ask for a *sconto* (discount).

Puppets
6 Tourist shops are full of puppets, varying in quality. Some craftsmen who produce puppets for performances also make puppets for sale as souvenirs, usually slightly smaller in scale than those used in the theatre. Antiques shops sell puppets too, but if it's the real item, expect to pay a high price.

Wine
7 Sicilian wines are coming into their own and there are lots of small producers making wines of excellent quality *(see pp72–3)*. Larger shops and vineyards will ship wines home for you.

Food
8 Unperishable food products allow you to bring a bit of Sicilian cuisine home. Most shops offer canned goods or items shrink-wrapped *(sotto vuoto)*. Look for olive oils and anything preserved in salt or oil such as tuna, olives, sundried tomatoes, capers and artichokes. There are good Sicilian cookbooks in English – look for Anna Tasca Lanza and Mary Taylor Simeti.

Fabric Items
9 In Novara di Sicilia you can find items handmade in wool felt, while Erice is known for woven rugs in geometric patterns. Hand-sewn items are available at antiques shops and at the linen stalls of markets.

Terracotta
10 Hand-moulded terracotta figurines have long played a part in the Nativity scene tradition, representing folks from all walks of life. You can find old figurines in antiques shops, and some craftsmen still make new ones using traditional methods.

If buying Sicilian wine to take home, check the regulations for shipping alcohol into your home country.

Left **Lifeguard patrol** Right **Beachside bar**

🔟 Tips for Families

1 Attitude To Kids
Italians love children – particularly Sicilians. Restaurants, bars, and hotels are eager to accommodate families and children, so there is no need to be shy about asking for special favours or services.

2 Accommodation
Resort villages have staff on hand to take care of children and entertain them with supervised group activities. Call ahead to find out the age groups provided for, as some holiday villages do not host activities for children under the age of 12.

3 Meals
Menus do not always include a separate section for children, but a *mezza porzione* (half portion) of pasta is usually available on request. For simple, non-spicy dishes, ask for *pasta con l'olio e formaggio* (a simple pasta dish with olive oil and cheese), *pasta al pomodoro* (with tomatoes), or *pasta/riso in bianco* (plain pasta or rice). Highchairs are generally available.

4 Water Safety
Only the larger and more populated beaches have *bagnini* (lifeguards), and if they do, there's a good chance that these flirtatious guys in tiny red swimsuits won't have their eyes on the water. Trained as they may be, it's a good idea to keep an eye on your kids yourself. The *alimentari* and souvenir shops that abound in most seaside villages sell all sorts of gear from flippers and snorkels to sun protection and floating boards.

5 Bathing
Almost every beach has at least one bar that rents beach equipment for beachgoers, including umbrellas, chairs and pedal boats. The larger establishments have convenient showers, changing rooms with lockers where you can leave all your family's beach belongings, a restaurant and a bar.

6 Extra Beds
You can usually add an extra bed or cot to a double hotel room for a 30 per cent surcharge. Many hotels, even so-called luxury hotels, expect families and have rooms outfitted with three, four or five beds as a matter of course, as well as extra space.

7 Going Out
Sicilian families stick together and often eat out in large groups, socializing in the piazza or making the *passeggiata (see p53)* until the early hours of the morning. As the summer drags on, the siesta gets longer and longer, meals start later and later, and you'll notice that local kids stay up until well after midnight.

8 Siesta
Take advantage of the afternoon siesta time to let children have a short nap. It's not a bad idea for the parents either. Most of Sicily shuts down during the hottest hours of the day, and comes to life again when the air cools off in the evening.

9 Illness
If you haven't brought the medicines you need with you, feel under the weather or need any medical advice while in Sicily, start with a visit to a pharmacy. Italian pharmacists are trained to diagnose and treat minor problems and can recommend paediatricians. Holiday villages and campsites have seasonal infirmaries and your consular agent should be able to provide a list of paediatricians who speak your language *(see p128)*.

10 Safety
Although water safety items are readily available, be sure to check in advance with your rental company or travel agency that child seats and bicycle helmets are available. If they are not, bring your own from home or hunt around for a company that includes them.

Left **Eating at the bar** Right **Market for picnic food**

🔟 Sicily on a Budget

1 Travel Discounts
Check with your travel agent for inexpensive tickets on charter airlines. All-inclusive packages are often a bargain, including airfare or boat fare, food, lodging and often car hire for one set price. These packages are often only available during the summer season.

2 Discounts
At the majority of sights and museums there are reduced entry fees for groups, students between the ages of 18 and 25, and free entry for those under 18 and over 65 (although sometimes this applies to EU citizens only). During Italian Culture Week in spring most state-run sites offer free entry to all.

3 Accommodation
Hostels and *pensioni*, particularly those run by religious orders *(see p145)*, offer inexpensive, safe and clean lodging. Take advantage of the Solé hotel chain where member hotels (2- and 3-stars) offer a 10 per cent discount to former clients. Get a stamp on your brochure and travel from member hotel to member hotel to get a discount throughout your entire stay. 🔊 *Catena Hotels del Sole: www. sicilyhotelsnet.it • info@ sicilyhotelsnet.it*

4 Restaurants
Unassuming *trattorie* serve up hearty helpings of traditional foods – a crowd of locals is a good sign of the quality. House wine costs less than the listed wines; meat costs less than fish. Unless you're famished, a first course and an *antipasto* or vegetable dish should be plenty, and is more affordable *(see p138)*.

5 Picnics
Scenic picnics are highly recommended and fit for any budget. *Alimentari* offer fresh, local salami, cheese and olives. Markets sell fresh fruits and vegetables, and bakeries and *alimentari* will make sandwiches to order. Wine is available at reasonable prices.

6 Bars and Rosticcerie
Sicily has a tradition of fast, filling food in bars and *rosticcerie*. Look for *panelle*, *arancini*, *sfincione*, pizza, and enjoy the variety of baked pastas and sandwiches. It costs less to eat at the bar than it does to sit at a table.

7 Low Season
Nicer hotels drop their prices considerably (as much as 40 per cent) before and after high season (July and August). The weather is nice and the water is good for swimming in June and September. For discounts in the high season, when people hit the coast, look to cities and towns. Some hotels lure people inland with cheap rates in the summer.

8 Public Transport
Take advantage of buses, which offer a full day pass for around €2.50. Tickets are sold at kiosks near bus stops, *tabacchi* (look for the black-and-white "T" sign) and in some bars, and must be validated upon entry in the bus. Do not throw tickets away, as you may be asked to prove you used them. Free bicycle rentals may be arranged at the tourist office in many areas.

9 Free Sites
Sicily is a living monument. The landscape, the smell of the sea, the lively markets, the medieval churches, fields rich with bounty, are proof that *la vita vera* (real life) is still going strong – these are among the finest things Sicily has to offer, and they are all free.

10 Museum Fees
A *biglietto cumulativo* (cumulative ticket) is a great way to save money. It's a one-price entry to several sights in the same area. However, you will have to request one, as the cashier at the ticket booth will not offer you one automatically.

Left **Bancomat ATM sign** Right **Automatic Exchange Machine**

🔟 Banking and Communications

1 Currency
Along with 11 other countries in the European Union, Italy adopted the euro as its common currency in January 2002. Check newspapers and currency services for up-to-date exchange rates.

2 Bureaux de Change
The best bet for getting a good rate when changing money is generally an Automatic Exchange Machine. Check with your bank at home to find out about any hidden charges. *Bureaux de change* are located in cities, but usually give a low rate of exchange and charge a high fee (and they close for lunch which can prove inconvenient). Banks generally charge lower fees but the queues can be insufferably long.

3 ATMs
ATMs *(Bancomat)* are usually offered by banks and are found all over Sicily, apart from remoter villages. Except for brief interruptions in service, they work 24 hours a day. The Italian banks don't usually charge a fee for using an ATM at their end, but your bank at home might charge a percentage for the transaction. Banks are most likely to charge a lower fee than a credit card company, whose fees for cash advances can be steep.

4 Credit cards
Credit cards are sometimes accepted, sometimes not. It's worth asking first or looking for the credit card symbol on the window of a shop or restaurant. Plan to pay for a good portion of your trip in cash, especially petrol. When credit cards are accepted, Visa and American Express are the most commonly used.

5 Travellers' Cheques
Travellers' cheques can be changed at hotels, banks and *bureaux de change*, but the rates for foreign exchange are not usually good.

6 Telephones
Public telephones can be found in city streets and some bars. They operate with phonecards purchased from *tabacchi* (tobacconists). Break off a corner to activate the card. Some small villages only have one hidden phone, so ask for *un telefono pubblico*. European mobile phones will have coverage except in very mountainous areas.

7 Internet
More and more Internet connection points are popping up on the island, usually in the cities and tourist areas, where you'll find a few Internet cafés similar to those now seen the world over. Hotels will often let you connect to the Internet from the reception desk.

8 Post
Italian post offices function like banks, and there are always extremely long and slow moving queues, especially at the end of the month when old age pensioners' cheques come in and electricity bills need to be paid. As with almost everything else, they also close for the extended lunchtime siesta. If you just need to purchase *francobolli* (stamps), save yourself the hassle and buy them from *tabacchi*.

9 Newspapers
US, British, French and German newspapers are available on newsstands in Palermo, Trapani, Catania and Messina. In the smaller villages and hinterlands, only tourist spots such as Taormina, the Aeolian Islands and Erice are likely to have any foreign newspapers on sale.

10 Television and Radio
Italian television is notoriously bad, old-fashioned and often sexist. Only the better hotels will have satellite television broadcasting foreign channels such as the BBC, CNN or SkyNews. Radio coverage is unreliable in the mountainous zones.

Left **Police car** Right **Sicilian pharmacy**

🔟 Security and Health

1 Emergency Numbers
The emergency telephone number for the *polizia* (police) is 113 and can be used to call an ambulance too. Call 115 to report a fire.

2 Police
Heavily-armed *carabinieri*, dressed in sleek red-striped pants, are usually staked out by the side of the road pulling over cars to check documentation or taking care of airport security. The local police *(polizia)* wear blue uniforms with their pistols in white holsters and are responsible for general security, safety and petty crime.

3 Insurance
Doctors and pharmacies *(farmacie)* provide receipts that are accepted by insurance companies back home but ask your insurance provider what additional information may be necessary. If your own health insurance does not provide coverage while you are travelling, ask your agent for additional travel insurance.

4 Pharmacies
Pharmacists are trained to diagnose and treat minor problems. Many items for sale, regardless of whether or not a doctor's prescription is required, are kept behind the counter in one of a thousand little drawers, so you usually have to ask for what you're looking for. Pointing to your sore throat is enough to let them know that you need lozenges, for example. A green cross signifies a pharmacy; if it's closed there should be an indication of the nearest one that's open posted on or near the shop door. Toiletries are also available in *profumerie*.

5 Hospitals
If you are in need of medical service in an emergency, *pronto soccorso* (first aid) is available at hospitals *(ospedale)*. In the remote interior, you'll have to ask for details of the nearest hospital, or dial the emergency number.

6 Dentists
Dental care is not great in Sicily and therefore not covered by most travel insurance policies. If you have a problem that needs immediate attention, ask the local pharmacist to recommend a dentist, or better yet, check with your consulate for a list of dentists who speak your language.

7 Theft
Although crime is not rampant, be aware of thieves, especially in crowded markets or piazzas. Report an incident to the police immediately, if necessary using the emergency number 113. You may need documentation from the police to show to your insurance company.

8 Coastguards
The *guardia costiera* patrol all of Italy's coastline. Among their other duties, they are responsible for controlling pleasure craft. Boats registered in a country within the EU are not subject to customs control, but must have on board all papers necessary for the countries where the boat and skipper are registered, and must follow laws pertaining to Italian waters. For an emergency at sea, call the coastguard emergency number, 1530.

9 Fire
Wild fires break out easily in the dry summer and spread rapidly blown by the hot *scirocco* wind. Call the Vigili del Fuoco at 115 to report a fire.

10 Water safety
Bagnini (lifeguards) are not always on duty at pools or beaches. There is no widespread use of the flag system, or wind and current signals. Although Sicily's waters are not particularly hazardous, it's a good idea to consider all swimming as "at your own risk". Call the coastguard in an emergency

Left **Open-air trattoria** Right **Antipasto**

Dining Out Tips

1 Restaurant Types
Restaurants vary from the inexpensive *tavola calda* (literally "hot table") to casual *pizzerie*, *osterie* and *trattorie*, to the more elegant *ristorante*. An enjoyable meal is an important part of Italian life, so feel free to linger in any establishment as long as you like.

2 Breakfast
Hotels serve good strong coffee and bread, if not a full buffet. Out and about, bars serve strong *espresso* or *cappuccino* early in the day, usually accompanied by a *cornetto* (croissant) or *arancini (see p71)*. The typical Sicilian breakfast is *gelato* in a brioche – a sweet but heavenly way to start the day.

3 Antipasto
Antipasto literally means "before the meal". It can be anything from salami and cheese, to marinated anchovies, or any creative little bite the chef has prepared.

4 Primo
This is the first course, and is usually a soup, pasta or rice cooked with vegetables, and some fish or meat. You can ask for a *mezza porzione* if you don't want a full plate of pasta. If you order cous cous with fish (a Sicilian speciality) it's often served as a *piatto unico* (single course) since it includes the pasta and fish on the same plate. *Primi* are eaten alone, with no vegetables, salad or bread.

5 Secondo
Second courses are based on meat or fish. A selection of grilled meats and *involtini* (slices of meat rolled around a stuffing) are usually on offer. Excellent fresh fish is available in almost every eatery on the island. The *secondo* is usually served alone on the plate, however, unlike the *primo*, it is perfectly acceptable to eat the course accompanied by bread and vegetables.

6 Contorni
Contorni are vegetable side dishes that accompany the *secondo*. They usually consist of salads, tomato salad, grilled vegetables or roasted potatoes, French fries or greens.

7 Cheese, Desserts and Coffee
After the main meal, you might be offered a cheese course. Ask for the speciality of the area. Fruit is almost always available. *Dolci* (desserts) in Sicily *(see p71)* are excellent and often made in-house. Finally, coffee is served at the end of every meal. If it's late and you'd prefer to avoid the caffeine, ask for your coffee to be *decaffinato* (decaffenated).

8 Tipping
Bills for meals include *il coperto* (a small cover charge) and sometimes a *servizio* (service charge) of around 10 per cent which will be marked on the bill. If service charges are not included, you aren't usually expected to leave a tip, although it's always a nice gesture. An Italian will usually leave a few euros in a *trattoria* if the service and food were good, or if it's a place they frequent regularly. They leave a little more in a restaurant.

9 Wine
You'll be offered the house wine in a half or full litre carafe. If you are at all interested in wines, take a look at the wine list as there are usually at least a few good bottles at decent prices. Try a *malvasia*, *moscato passito*, or Marsala with cheese or dessert, or as an after-dinner drink.

10 Bars
All Sicilian bars serve coffee, pastries and sandwiches, specialities such as *arancini*, as well as beer, wine, *spumante* (sparkling wine) and a range of other alcoholic beverages. They are open from early in the morning until late at night. As a rule of thumb, it is always more expensive to eat or drink seated at a table than it is to stand at the bar.

Left & Right **Typical Sicilian hotels**

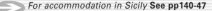

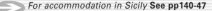Streetsmart

TOP 10 Accommodation Tips

1 Hotels
In popular areas such as Taormina and the cities hotels are more plentiful. Some hotels catering to business people are being opened, providing service more in line with what the Americans, British and western Europeans are used to. However, in the interior there's not much to choose from. If you want to stay in a certain area, you may need to find a hotel in the nearest large town.

2 Grading
Hotels are graded according to a star system, from one to five. One-star hotels are inexpensive and offer a choice of rooms with or without bath. Two- and three-star hotels are functional and are usually clean. Four-star hotels have added comforts such as swimming pools and modern bathrooms. The very few five-star hotels on the island are luxurious.

3 Reservations
Always book in advance in high season (July and August), but outside of these months you can usually book just a day or two ahead. Booking via telephone or fax is your best option; although many hotels now have e-mail addresses, they are not always checked regularly. The staff at hotel reception

desks usually speak enough foreign languages to make and confirm reservations.

4 High and Low Season
High season is July and August and most room rates go up during that time. Expect to pay more for rooms on the off-shore islands and at popular resorts such as Taormina. Some hotels also require a *mezza pensione* (half board) deal during high season. Prices drop as much as 40 per cent outside of high season.

5 Villas
Several foreign companies offer homes for rent, from country-side villas and seaside homes to apartments in a city or town. For a small group or family, renting a house can be economical but make sure you check the insurance cover carefully.

6 Farms
There has been an explosion of agritourism in the last few years in Sicily and there is a wide range of quality and services. Some offer tranquil private accommodation or apartment rentals on small farms; others have accommodation with the option to get involved in the working activities, such as picking grapes.
✪ www.agriturist.it

7 Camping
There are plenty of campsites along Sicily's coastline and a few inland, rated with a star system like hotels and usually well-equipped with swimming pools, *pizzerie*, bars, beach facilities, and occasionally an infirmary in high season. Pitching a tent outside of official campsites is not allowed.
✪ www.camping.it

8 Half Board
In high season some agritourism and resort hotels require that you take half board, which means breakfast and one other meal included in the price of your room. Some offer *pensione completo* (full board).

9 Private Rooms
Private rooms for rent are available in most tourist areas, particularly the offshore islands, at Cefalù and Taormina. You'll usually have more than your fair share to choose from disembarking from a hydrofoil or in train stations. Tourist offices and travel agencies also have listings.

10 Hostels
Much cheaper than traditional hotel rooms, hostels also provide local information, laundry and kitchen facilities, television and Internet access. Some have bars and offer room rates with breakfast or other meals.

For accommodation in Sicily **See pp140–47**

Left **Eremo della Giubiliana** Right **Grand Hotel Villa Igea**

TOP10 Luxury Hotels

1 Eremo della Giubiliana, Ragusa

Knights of St John en route to Malta took refuge in this 15th-century fortified monastic building and it is still offering elegant refuge to travellers. With just 11 rooms, each guest is treated to the most attentive service. Rooms, public areas and grounds are authentically restored with wood and iron furnishings, fountains and stone courts. Excellent restaurant and garden with pool. ◎ *Contrada Giubiliana* • *Map F5* • *0932 66 91 19* • *www. eremodellagiubiliana.it* • *Dis. access* • *€€€€€*

2 Grand Hotel Baia Verde, Catania

The 158 brightly decorated rooms, each with living area and a terrace, surround the palm-planted pool area and look out to the Ionian Sea. ◎ *Via Angelo Musco 8, Cannizzaro* • *Map G4* • *095 491 522* • *www. baiaverde.it* • *€€€€€*

3 Grand Hotel Timeo & Villa Flora, Taormina

The Timeo takes full advantage of its site, nestled into the bougainvillea and palm-covered hillside just beneath the ancient theatre. The 46 rooms are decorated in grand Baroque style. The bar and restaurant occupy magical terraces with amazing views. ◎ *Via Teatro Greco 59* • *Map H3* • *0924 23 801* • *www.framon-hotels.it* • *€€€€€*

4 San Domenico Palace, Taormina

Built as a monastery in the 1400s, the structure now houses 100 rooms. In beautiful grounds, the San Domenico offers views of the bay and Mount Etna, tennis courts, a pool and gym. ◎ *Piazza San Domenico 5* • *Map H3* • *0924 613 111* • *www.thi.it* • *Dis. access* • *€€€€€*

5 Grand Hotel Villa Igea, Palermo

Art Nouveau master Ernesto Basile built this grand villa at the end of the 19th century on the slopes of Monte Pellegrino. It is now Palermo's premier luxury hotel. Dine on the terraces overlooking the sea. ◎ *Salita Belmonte 43* • *Map L2* • *091 54 37 44* • *www.thi.it* • *Dis. access* • *€€€€€*

6 Hotel Principe di Villafranca, Palermo

This new hotel caters to business travellers. The 34 rooms are individually decorated. The hotel offers a gym, restaurant, parking and in-room internet access. ◎ *Via G. Turrisi Colonna 4* • *Map J1* • *091 611 8523* • *www. principedivillafranca.it* • *€€€€*

7 Grand Hotel, Syracuse

Built as a hotel in the 1800s and restored in 1995, the rooms are elegant and have views of the old centre and the sea. A shuttle bus leads to a private beach. ◎ *Viale Mazzini 12* • *Map H5* • *0931 464 600* • *www. grandhotelsr.it* • *Dis. access* • *€€€€€*

8 Grand Hotel Villa Politi, Syracuse

This villa was built in 1862 in Art Nouveau style and was converted almost immediately into a 100-room hotel. Guests enjoy a pool and quick access to Syracuse's archaeological sites and museum. ◎ *Via M. Politi 2* • *Map H5* • *0931 412 121* • *www.villapoliti.com* • *€€€€*

9 Excelsior Palace Hotel, Taormina

This 4-star hotel is notable for the views of Mount Etna and for the gardens with swimming pool on a promontory overlooking the lovely Bay of Naxos. ◎ *Via Toselli 8* • *Map H3* • *0924 23 975* • *€€€€€*

10 Centrale Palace Hotel, Palermo

An elegant, restored *palazzo* with marble-clad public areas. There is a roof terrace for dinner. ◎ *Corso Vittorio Emanuele 327* • *Map L5* • *091 33 66 66* • *cphotel@tin.it* • *Dis. access* • *€€€€€*

Note: Unless otherwise stated, all hotels accept credit cards, and have en-suite bathrooms and air conditioning

Price Categories

For a standard, double room per night (with breakfast if included), taxes and extra charges.

€	under €50
€€	€50–€100
€€€	€100–€150
€€€€	€150–€200
€€€€€	over €200

Above **Foresteria Baglio della Luna**

🔟 Historic Hotels

1 Foresteria Baglio della Luna, Agrigento

Guests are made to feel at home in this restored 13th-century tower and 18th-century *baglio*. The bright, intimate, central courtyard leads onto terraces shaded by olive and fruit trees with views to Agrigento's famed temples *(see pp26–9)*. Rooms on the upper level are furnished with antiques. Excellent restaurant *(see p115)*. ◈ Contrada Maddalusa, Valle de Templi • Map D4 • 0922 511 061 • €€€€€

2 Hotel Relais Modica

This renovated *palazzo* opened in 2002. There are lovely views of Modica, a terrace and family rooms. The service is friendly, too. ◈ Via Tommaso Campanella 99 • Map G6 • 0932 754 451 • €€

3 Hotel Belvedere, Taormina

Built as a grand hotel in 1902 on Taormina's hill-side, renovations have preserved the charm of the original while modernizing the guest rooms (most of them have good views). The Belvedere is also noted for its gardens with citrus and palm trees and serves pool-side lunches. ◈ Via Bagnoli Croci, 79 Map H3 • 0942-23 791 • www.villabelvedere.it • €€€

4 Katane Palace Hotel, Catania

This 58-room 4 star hotel in a restored *palazzo* opened in 2002. Modern rooms are comfortable, soundproofed and equipped with fax and modem access. The hotel offers parking, an airport shuttle and a restaurant serving Sicilian cuisine *(see p107)*. ◈ Via Finocchiaro Aprile 110 • Map G4 • 095 747 0702 • www.katanepalace.it • Dis. access • €€€

5 Domus Aurea, Agrigento

A villa dating from the 1800s was faithfully renovated in 2002 in Neo-Gothic style with Arab-inspired gardens and fountains. ◈ Contrada Maddalusa, Valle de Templi • Map D4 • 0922 511 061 • €€€€€

6 Atelier sul Mare, Castel di Tusa

It's not the building that is historic here, but the rooms themselves. Each room is an installation piece created by a modern artist, with evolving designs that guests are asked to participate in. Each room has a sea-front terrace. Within easy reach of Cefalù, the Madonie mountains and the Fiumara d'Arte sculpture garden. ◈ Via Cesare Battisti 4 • Map E2 • 0921 334 295 • www.ateliersulmare.it • No air conditioning • €€€

7 Baglio Santacroce, Erice

This 17th-century *baglio* sits on the slopes below Erice. Rooms are laid out around the stone court-yard and boast original stone walls, exposed wood beams, terracotta floors and traditional rugs. ◈ Valderice • Map B2 • 0923 891 111 • No air conditioning • €€

8 Baglio Conca d'Oro, Palermo

Located between Palermo and Monreale, in what is known as the "Golden Valley". The spacious rooms have terracotta and majolica tiled floors. ◈ Via Aquino 19c, Borgo Molara • Map D2 • 091 640 6286 • Dis. access • €€€

9 Massimo Plaza, Palermo

In a renovated *palazzo*. Rooms are soundproofed and take in the views of the piazza. Parking. ◈ Via Maqueda 437 • Map L4 • 091 32 56 57 • www.massimoplazahotel.com • €€€

10 Grand Hotel et des Palmes, Palermo

Built in Art Nouveau style in the mid-1800s. There are columned and marble public spaces where mafia dons once held meetings, although the rooms are less luxurious. ◈ Via Roma 398 • Map L3 • 091 602 8111 • www.thi.it • Dis. access • €€€€

Left **Alceste** Right **Hotel President**

🔟 Comfortable Hotels

1 Hotel Sport Club Portorais, Palermo
Minutes from Palermo airport, but this is not a typical airport hotel. There are ample, airy public spaces, modern rooms, a gym, a nice pool area, private beach, bar and restaurant. ◎ *Via Piraineto 125, Carini • Map D2 • 091 869 3481 • Dis. access • €€€*

2 Hotel Pomara, San Michele di Ganzaria
One of the most comfortable options inland. The location is rustic and affords excellent views of the rolling, wheat-covered hills but the family-run hotel is modern. Great views from the pool, excellent restaurant on site, and convenient for visiting Enna, Piazza Armerina, Morgantina and Caltagirone. ◎ *Via Vittorio Veneto 84 • Map F4 • 0933 976 976 • www. hotelpomara.com • Dis. access • €€*

3 Hotel Posta, Palermo
Recently renovated, this 2-star hotel is an excellent bargain choice in Palermo. The 27 rooms are large and clean, the public areas are equipped with a TV, parking is available, and there is free entry to a private beach in Mondello. Near the church of San Domenico. ◎ *Via Gagini 77 • Map L3 • 091 587 338 • €€*

4 Al Madarig, Castellammare del Golfo
A super comfortable 3-star hotel. Rooms have refrigerators, modern baths and shuttered geranium-clad windows overlooking the Gulf of Castellammare. A good base for visiting north-west Sicily. ◎ *Piazza Petrolo 7 • Map C2 • 0924 335 33 • almadarig@tin.it • €€*

5 Hotel del Corso, Taormina
A family-run, 3-star hotel recommended by locals, with good views. The newly renovated modern rooms have small terraces looking over the hillside, the Bay of Naxos and Mount Etna. Parking is also available. ◎ *Corso Umberto I, 238 • Map H3 • 0942 628 698 • hoteldelcorso@tiscalinet.it • €€€*

6 Nuovo Hotel Russo, Trapani
Part of the Sole hotel chain, in an excellent location in Trapani's historic centre. The hotel resembles a grandmother's living room despite a recent makeover. Rooms are serviceable and clean. Reserve a parking space in their tiny garage for a small fee. They usually encourage you to go out for breakfast, which is a joy in lively Trapani. ◎ *Via Tintori 4 • Map B2 • 0923 221 66 • €€*

7 Hotel Airone, Zafferana Etnea
A good base for Mount Etna excursions. In the pine woods above Zafferana Etnea, this 3-star hotel is built in mountain style, with nicely furnished rooms and an open dining room. They can arrange excursions up the volcano, horseriding and golf. ◎ *Via Cassone 67 • Map G3 • 095 708 1819 • www.hotel-airone.it • €€*

8 Hotel President, Marsala
A new, ultra-modern 124-room hotel with swimming pool, convention rooms and beach access. Good value for all the facilities included. ◎ *Via Nino Bixio 1 • Map B3 • 0923 999 333 • Dis. access • €€*

9 Albergo Aegusa, Favignana
Modern rooms, a terrace, a small garden restaurant and easy access to the beach. ◎ *Via Garibaldi 11, Favignana • Map A3 • 0923 922 430 • Dis. access • €€€*

10 Alceste, Selinunte
Another Sole hotel, the Alceste is a reasonably priced, family-run establishment in the quiet fishing village at Selinunte. Breakfast is served on a terrace with a beautiful view overlooking the sea. ◎ *Via Alceste 21 • Map B4 • 0924 46 184 • €€*

Note: *Unless otherwise stated, all hotels accept credit cards, and have en-suite bathrooms and air conditioning*

Above **Azienda Agrituristico La Perciata**

Price Categories

For a standard, double room per night (with breakfast if included), taxes and extra charges.

€	under €50
€€	€50–€100
€€€	€100–€150
€€€€	€150–€200
€€€€€	over €200

🔟 Agriturismo and B&Bs

1 Rosemarie Tasca d'Almerita's, Vallelunga

Rosemarie Tasca d'Almerita opens her home on the family's wine estate as a B&B. Relax on her rose-planted terraces, walk through the vineyards and tour the winery. Three bedrooms, two with private baths. ✪ Tenuta Regaleali • Map E3 • 091 583 132 • www.sicilyathome.com • No credit cards • No air conditioning • €€€

2 Tenuta Gangivecchio

The estate deep in the Madonie mountains was founded as an abbey in 1363 but has been in the Tornabene family since 1856. Choose from a private cottage or one of 8 rooms in the converted stables. A pool, cookery classes, hiking and horseriding. ✪ Contrada Gangivecchio, follow the signs from Gangi • Map E3 • 0921 689 191 • www.gangivecchio.it • No air conditioning • €€€

3 Azienda Agrituristica Tempio di Monte Jato

This villa was confiscated from a Mafia boss. Facilities now include a pool, horseback riding, and the opportunity to participate in the grape harvest. ✪ San Cipirello, Monte Jato • Map C2 • 349 853 6082 • tempiodimontejato@tiscali.it • Dis. access • €€€

4 Feudo Tudia

On a noble estate in heart of Sicily are 250 hectares of vines, olives, orchards and forest. From the outside it looks like a crumbling villa, but within are modern apartments with kitchenettes, dining room with stone arches, pool and tennis courts. ✪ Borgo Tudia, Commune di Castellana Sicula • Map E3 • 0934 673 029 • www.tudia.it • No air conditioning • €€

5 Azienda Agrituristico La Perciata, Syracuse

The estate produces figs, strawberries and olive oil, while the 4-star hotel rooms and apartments with terracotta floors and kitchenettes are grouped around tranquil gardens. Pool, tennis courts and horseback riding. ✪ Via Spinagallo 77, provincial road 14 from Syracuse to Canicattini • Map H5 • 0931 717 366 • www.perciata.il • Dis. access • €€

6 Azienda Agricola Fattoria Mosè

Choose from self-catering apartments with private terrace or a B&B option on Chiara Agnellos' working farm. Buildings open onto courtyards perfumed with jasmine and honeysuckle. Minimum two night stay. ✪ Via M. Pascal 4, Villaggio Mosè • Map D4 • 0922 606 115 • www.fattoriamose.com • No air conditioning • €€

7 Azienda Agrituristica Limoneto, Syracuse

The owners offer eight apartments equipped with refrigerators, as well as a children's playground, home-cooked meals, and excursions to Syracuse. ✪ Road 14 for Canicattini Bagni • Map H5 • 0931 717 352 • Dis. access • No credit cards • No air conditioning • €€

8 Casa Migliaca

A 17th-century estate with stone buildings, terraces and organic farm. ✪ Pettineo (between Cefalù and Santo Stefano di Camastra) • Map E2 • 0921 336 722 • www.casamigliaca.com • No air conditioning • €€

9 L'Acanto, Ortygia

A small hotel in the heart of Ortygia island, in Syracuse. Rooms are spacious and nicely decorated, some with terraces. Parking is available. ✪ Via Roma 15, Syracuse • Map H5 • 0931 46 11 29 • www.bebsicilia.it • €€

10 Azienda Agrituristica Bergi, Castelbuono

In Madonie mountain country, this organic farm produces fruit, vegetables and olives. Outbuildings house 14 guest rooms. ✪ Contrada Bergi • Map E3 • 0921 67 20 45 • www.agriturismobergi.com • Dis. access • No air conditioning • €€

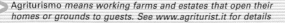

Agriturismo *means working farms and estates that open their homes or grounds to guests. See www.agriturist.it for details*

143

Left **Coasthouse Residences** Right **Il Pescatore**

ᴛᴏᴘ10 Self-Catering and Villas

1 Azienda Agrituristica Villa Levante, Castelbuono

Three nicely restored self-catering apartments are set in the towers of a 19th-century castle with crenellated towers, stained glass, pretty gardens and a farm producing olive oil. Mountain bike and hike on marked trails or walk in to Castelbuono. ✪ *Via Isnello • Map E3 • 0921 67 19 14 • www. agriturismosicilia.com • €€*

2 Residenza d'Aragona, Palermo

Nicely furnished, modern apartments in the heart of uptown Palermo between Teatro Massimo and the Politeama. Twenty suites are housed in a newly restored 19th-century *palazzo* and are all outfitted with a living room and small kitchen. ✪ *Via Ottavio d'Aragona 25 • Map L2 • 091 66 22 222 • Dis. access • €€€€*

3 Enza Marturano, Lipari

In the centre of Lipari, not far from the Marina Corta *(see p12)*. Four bright private rooms are grouped around a communal sitting room, kitchen and terrace. Enza, the owner, is very friendly and can make recommendations for excursions. ✪ *Via Maurolico 35 • Map G1 • 090 981 2544 • No credit cards • €*

4 Il Pescatore, Selinunte

In a family home in the fishing village of Selinunte. Seven rooms share kitchen facilities and two terraces, one for dining, the other with a view of the temples and laundry facilities. ✪ *Via Castore e Polluce 31, Localita Marinella di Selinunte • Map B4 • 0924 46 303 • No credit cards • No air conditioning • €*

5 Coast House Residences

Apartments for rent in the Kalura area to the east of Cefalù, with clear blue water and rock formations. The apartments are built on a cliff side, with shady terraces and a path down to the small private beach. ✪ *C/o Gestioni Immobiliari di Bonomo Giovanna, G.P. Presitisione 4, Cefalù • Map E2 • 0921 922 339 • gestionimmobiliari@kefa.it • €€€*

6 The Parker Company

This reputable company offers more than 25 properties in Sicily, from cottages to castles that sleep from 2 to 17 people. They occasionally have representatives on site, help plan itineraries, secure hire cars, and organize day trips. ✪ *Seaport Landing, 152 The Lynnway, Lynn, MA 01902, USA • 781 596-8282 • www.theparkercompany. com*

7 Cuendet

This Italian/Swiss company has 28 years' experience renting villas worldwide. Choose from 31 properties in Sicily, from farmhouses to villas to apartments in castles. ✪ *Cuendet, Strada di Strove 17, Monteriggioni, Italy • 0577 576 330 • www.cuendet.com*

8 Internet Villas Inc

Another company with more than 20 properties on Sicily and Pantelleria, and they provide assistance with car and mobile phone rentals, on or off-site catering services and winery tours. ✪ *8 Knight St, Suite 205, Norwalk, CT 06851, USA • 203 855-8161 • www.italianvillas.com*

9 Rentvillas.com

For 18 years this agency has been renting European properties, and they offer more than 50 options in Sicily. They can assist with travel plans and cooking schools. ✪ *700 E Main St, Ventura, CA 93001, USA • 805 641-1650 • www.rentvillas.com*

10 Group Travel

Assists with accommodation in Italy specializing in meeting clients' individual needs. More than 40 properties in Sicily. ✪ *C/o Group Travel Enterprises, Inc., 2400 Bluff Creek Drive, Columbia, MO 65201, USA • 1-800 917 2725 • www. travel-italy.com*

Above **Lido Azzuro**

🔟 Pensione and Monasteries

1 Pocho Residence Isulidda, San Vito lo Capo

Nice small *pensione* with nine clean, modern rooms, wooden furniture and amazing views of Monte Cofano and the gulf. They offer a cooking course, arrange airport transfers, horseback riding, tour guides, and boat and diving excursions. The restaurant is famous for its cous cous dishes *(see p97).*
⊗ *Contrada Makari*
• *Map B2* • *0923 97 25 25*
• *Dis. access* • *€€*

2 Pensione Tranchina, Scopello

A 10-room *pensione* in this tiny fishing village. Rooms are nicely decorated with iron or wooden bedsteads, and several have a view of the sea. The ground floor sitting area has an open fireplace and the owners cook excellent Sicilian cuisine, mostly fresh seafood and vegetables from their garden.
⊗ *Via A Diaz 7* • *Map C2*
• *0924 541 099* • *No air conditioning* • *€€*

3 Hotel Victoria, Taormina

A 2-star *pensione.* The breakfast room has a terrace and view down onto the Corso. Rooms are comfortable and there are 3 parking spots. ⊗ *Corso Umberto 81* • *Map H3* • *0942 23 372*
• *€€*

4 Lido Azzuro, Selinunte

The rooms in this small *pensione* on Selinunte's promenade are clean, cheerfully decorated and serviceable, some with terraces. There's a front porch for sitting out to watch the *passeggiata,* and a discount on meals at the owners' restaurant across the street. ⊗ *Via Marco Polo 98* • *Map B4*
• *0924 46 256* • *No air conditioning* • *€*

5 L'Arca, Noto

Small, four-room *pensione* in the heart of Noto's historic centre, in a private courtyard (you enter through an arch, hence the name). Great location, serviceable rooms and helpful staff.
⊗ *Via Rocco Pirri 14/8*
• *Map G5* • *0931 838 656*
• *Dis. access* • *No credit cards* • *€€*

6 La Giarra, Cefalù

This *pensione* in Cefalù's historic centre has undergone a major renovation. Rooms are equipped with TVs and air conditioning, and some have a terrace with a view down the narrow streets and to the sea.
⊗ *Via Veterani 40* • *Map E2*
• *0921 421 562* • *Dis. access* • *€€*

7 Albergo Domus Mariae, Syracuse

The Ursuline sisters run a hotel in a restored 19th-century *palazzo* on Ortygia. Some of the modern 18 rooms offer air conditioning and a sea view. Books up quickly.
⊗ *Via Vittorio Veneto 76, Syracuse* • *Map H5* • *0931 248 54* • *€€€*

8 Monastero di San Benedetto, Noto

Benedictine sisters welcome you to their 17th-century monastery. Rooms are modern, large and clean, and most have baths. A 10:30pm curfew.
⊗ *Via dei Mille 106–108*
• *Map G5* • *0931 891 2255*
• *No credit cards* • *No air conditioning* • *€*

9 Casa dell'Accoglienza Don Giustino by the Padri Vocazionisti

About 16 km (12 miles) from Agrigento in a little seaside village. The modern hotel, run by priests, sits right on the beach, and many rooms have a terrace. Simple restaurant, bar and parking. ⊗ *Via Principe di Piemonte 1, Siculiana Marina* • *Map D4* • *0922 815 210* • *Dis. access* • *No credit cards* • *No air conditioning* • *€*

10 Albergo Don Bosco Emmaus, Zafferana Etnea

This large modern building sits in the forest above Zafferana Etnea. Many of the furnished rooms have terraces and views of Mount Etna or the sea. ⊗ *Via Cassone 75*
• *Map G3* • *095 708 1888*
• *Dis. access* • *€*

Left **Club Med Kamarina** Right **Club Med Cefalù**

Resort Hotels

1 Raya, Panarea

A study in total relaxation, where white-washed buildings with large terraces look out over the island to the sea. There are no elevators, televisions, cars or street lights, but the reception area includes a bar, disco and restaurant, the latter serving fresh fish dinners on a terrace lit with oil lamps. The staff can arrange excursions. ® *Via San Pietro • Map G1 • 090 983 013 • www.netnet.it/ hotel/raya/index • Closed Nov–Feb • €€€€€*

2 Hotel Signum, Salina

A lovely location on a vine-covered hillside. Thirty rooms equipped with ceiling fans are set in a typical Aeolian house and outbuildings. White-washed walls surround terraces looking down to the sea. The restaurant is highly recommended. ® *Via Scalo, 15, Malfa • Map G1 • 090 98 44 375 • www.netnet.it/Salina/ Signum • €€€€*

3 Hotel Santa Isabel, Salina

A gorgeous small hotel on a hillside. Each of the 10 two-level suites has a refrigerator and living room with views down to the sea, and is decorated in minimal Aeolian style with terracotta floors, whitewashed walls and bright furniture. There's a large terrace for outdoor dining on a cliff over the sea, and beach access via a path down the hill. ® *Via Scalo, 12, Malfa • Map G1 • 090 98 44 018 • www.santaisabel. isole-eolie.it • €€*

4 Hotel Villa Meligunis, Lipari

The bright rooms at this 4-star hotel have terraces and sea views. The hotel offers a restaurant, gardens, pool, shuttles to Lipari's beaches and assistance with excursions. ® *Via Marte 7 • Map G1 • 090 981 2426 • www.netnet.it/ villameligunis • €€€€*

5 Hotel Villa Sant'Andrea, Taormina

Rooms with terraces and sea views are housed in a restored 19th-century villa beneath Monte Tauro. There is dining under the palm trees and a private beach at Mazzarò. ® *Via Nazionale, 137, Mazzarò • Map H3 • 0942 23 125 • www.framon-hotels.it • €€€€€*

6 Kalura Hotel, Cefalù

This large modern hotel offers 65 rooms and a range of facilities, including a private beach, pool, tennis, billiards, darts, mountain bikes, canoes, scuba diving, sailing, horse riding, dance classes and guided tours. ® *Via Vincenzo Cavallaro 13 • Map E2 • 0921 421 354 • www.kalura.it • €€€*

7 Hotel Capo San Vito, San Vito lo Capo

This modern 4-star hotel has wood floors, terraces and sea views. A private beach has lounge chairs and umbrellas for guests. ® *Via San Vito 1 • Map B2 • 0923 97 21 2 • www. caposanvito.it • €€€€*

8 Tonnara di Bonagia, Tracino

This large hotel and congress centre is built around a 16th-century *baglio* below Erice. There are 47 rooms and 55 apartments, a pool and private beach. ® *Contrada Sopra Portella 28 • Map B2 • 0923 431 111 • www. framon-hotels.com • Dis. access • €€€€*

9 Club Med Kamarina, Scoglitti

A Club Med village with 149 rooms and 529 bungalows. Facilities include restaurants, bars, tennis, windsurfing, sailing, a spa, volleyball and children's activities. ® *BP 25-97 100 • Map F5 • 0932 91 91 11 • www.clubmed. com • Dis. access • €€€*

10 Club Med Cefalù

A holiday village with 496 straw huts. Activities include swimming, volleyball and a gym. Bring your own towels and a padlock for the hut. ® *Santa Lucia • Map E2 • 0921 423 977 • www.clubmed.com • Dis. access • No en-suite bathrooms • €€€*

Note: *Unless otherwise stated, all hotels accept credit cards, and have en-suite bathrooms and air conditioning*

Above **Oasi di Selinunte**

Price Categories

For a standard, double room per night (with breakfast if included), taxes and extra charges.

€ under €50
€€ €50–€100
€€€ €100–€150
€€€€ €150–€200
€€€€€ over €200

Campsites and Hostels

1 Ostello per la Gioventù Etna, Nicolosi

A large hostel on the slopes of Mount Etna, at 700 m (2,300 ft) above sea level. There are 70 beds, a number of small bathrooms and special rooms for families. Also a restaurant and bar. ✆ Via della Quercia 7 • Map G3 • 095 791 4686 • etna hostel@hotmail.com • €

2 Ostello per la Gioventù G Amodeo, Erice

Located about 4 km (2.5 miles) from Trapani at the beginning of the steep hill up to Erice. It is a new, rather institutional hostel but with helpful staff, 52 rooms, small bathrooms, a restaurant, and a view out over the Egadi Islands. ✆ Map B2 • 0923 552 964 • scral. erice-touring@libero.it • €

3 Ostello per la Gioventù Ulisse, Taormina

This small hostel has a planted terrace with sea views, 20 beds in regular and family rooms, kitchen facilities, bar and restaurant. ✆ Vico San Francesco di Paola 9 • Map H3 • 0942 23 193 • ostelloulisse. taormina@email.it • €

4 Residence Baja Guidaloca, Scopello

This residence provides small bungalows that can accommodate any size of group, each with kitchenette and terrace. The park-like setting includes terraces under olive trees. Near the beach. ✆ Guidaloca, Scopello • Map C2 • 0924 31 872 • www.sicilia. indettaglio it • €

5 Oasi di Selinunte

This classic Italian holiday villaggio offers 89 spots for tents and caravans and a 30-room hotel. Activities include swimming pools, beach access at Selinunte, tennis, soccer, basketball and volleyball. Restaurant on site. ✆ Via Pitagora, Marinella di Selinunte • Map B4 • 0924 46 885 • oasiselinunte@tiscalinet.it • No credit cards • €

6 Camping Il Forte, Pachino

This camping village is near the sandy beach at Marzamemi with 250 camping spots, 12 rooms, 32 apartments and 32 bungalows. Facilities include public telephones, infirmary, restaurant, bar and market. Activities include children's games, tennis, volleyball, waterskiing and beach access. ✆ Marzamemi • Map G6 • 0931 841 011/132 • www. fortevillage.net • Dis. access • €

7 Camping Village Kameni, Ribera

This campsite by the sea provides 160 tent and caravan spots, adult and children's pool, tennis, restaurant and beach access. ✆ C/da Cameni Superiore, Seccagrande, Ribera • Map C4 • 0925 69 212 • Dis. access • €

8 Camping Village Internazionale San Leone, Agrigento

A 3-star camping village with 300 camping spots and 120 rooms with terraces. Activities include a pool, tennis, volleyball, a sandy beach; restaurant, infirmary and camper service. ✆ Loc. Le Dune 92100 • Map D4 • 0922 416 121 • Dis. access • €€€

9 Camping Baia del Sole, Ragusa

This 4-star holiday village along the sandy coast at Marina di Ragusa offers 100 camping spots, a 20-room hotel, 5 apartments and 14 bungalows. Facilities include a restaurant, bar, swimming pools, playground, tennis, volleyball and beach access. ✆ Marina Ragusa-Lungomare 97100 • Map F5 • 0932 239844 • www.baiadelsole.it • €

10 Camping Costa Ponente, Cefalù

A 3-star campsite with spots for tents and caravans, swimming pool, tennis and access to the beach below. Facilities include a bar, self-service restaurant and a small market. ✆ Loc. Ogliatrillo, state road 113 at km 190 • Map E2 • 0921 420085 • No credit cards • €

General Index

Index

Acknowledgements

Main Contributor
Elaine Trigiani is a Sicilian-American art historian. Having worked in Sicily, she now conducts archival research, leads tours and writes about art history and food from her home in Tuscany.

Produced by Sargasso Media Ltd, London

Editorial Director
Zoë Ross
Art Editor
Janis Utton
Editor
John Sinclair
Picture Research
Helen Stallion
Proofreader
Stewart J Wild
Indexer
Hilary Bird
Editorial Assistance
Louis Mendola

Main Photographers
Demetrio Carrasco & Nigel Hicks

Illustrator
chrisorr.com

FOR DORLING KINDERSLEY
Publisher
Douglas Amrine
Senior Designer
Ian Midson

Senior Editor
Lucinda Cooke
Senior Cartographic Editor
Casper Morris
DTP
Jason Little
Production
Melanie Dowland

Maps John Plumer

Special Assistance
The author would like to thank the following people for their assistance:
Corrado Assenza, Mark Canizzaro, Robert Canizzaro, Paul Canizzaro, Leonardo Canizzaro, Francesca Canizzaro, Carmela Como, Jean and Jim Enochs, Giuseppe Grappolini, Nino Norrito, Dell and Gianni Palazzolo, Kate Papacosmos, Mike Sacks, Giovanni Saladino, Mariella Sciacca, David Perin Trigiani

Picture Credits
t-top; tc top centre; tr top right; cla-centre left above; ca-centre above; cra-centre right above; cl-centre left; c-centre; cr-centre right; clb-centre left below; cb-centre below; crb-centre right below; bl-below left; bc-below centre; br-below right.

Acknowledgements

Every effort has been made to trace the copyright holders, and we apologize in advance for any unintentional omissions. We would be pleased to insert the appropriate acknowledgements in any subsequent edition of this publication.

The publishers would like to thank the following individuals, companies, and picture libraries for permission to reproduce their photographs:

AGF/Sintesi: 131 tl

Franco Barbagallo/Grazia Neri: 21c, 21b, 53t, 58tl, 59, 105tr, 131tr; Barocco Winery: 72c

Canali Photobank: 43r, 60tl, 60b, 114tl; Cephas/Alan Proust: 58tr,73r, Mick Rock: 72tl, 72tr; Club Med: 146tl, 146tr, Carlo Columba/Il Dagherrotipo: 56tr, 57t; Corbis: 1, 4–5, 16t, 16–17, 17t, 17c, 17b, 33b, 34–5, 36tl, 36tr, 36b, 37r, 43t, 44b, 60tr, 78–9, 84–5, 90tl, 102–103, 104tr, 120–21, 124tl, 124tr,

Cristaldifilm/ Films Ariane/Kobal Collection: 61r

Andrea Getuli/Il Dagherrotipo: 24–25, 108c

INDEX/Alberti: 111l; INDEX/Baldi: 92b; INDEX/ Firenze: 13cr, 61t

Willi La Farina/Il Dagherrotipo: 56tl

NHPA: 132tr

Giovanni Rinaldi/Il Dagherrotipo: 25cr, 30-31, 42tl, 42b, 56b, 58b, 109t

Sanvitocouscous.com: 57r; Antonio Zimbone: 16b, 104tl.

Front Cover: DK Picture Library: John Heseltine tc, cla, bl; Clive Streeter clb; Robert Harding Picture Library: Michael Newton main image. Back Cover: DK Picture Library: John Heseltine tl, tc, tr.

All other images are © Dorling Kindersley. For further information see: www.dkimages.com

Special Editions

Top 10 Guides can be purchased in bulk quantities at discounted prices. Personalized jackets and excerpts can also be tailored to meet your needs. Please contact (in the UK) – Sarah.Burgess@dk.com or Special Sales, Dorling Kindersley Ltd, 80 Strand, London WC2R 0RL; (in the US) – Special Markets Department, DK Publishing, Inc., 375 Hudson Street, New York, NY 10014.